823.7 Gre
Gregory, Fiona
Jane Austen's Pride and prejudice
/

34028083448697
CC $9.95   ocn434379191
              07/29/13

Insight Stu

Fi   7

Pride and Prejudice

Jane Austen

insight

insight

Jane Austen's Pride and Prejudice by Fiona Gregory
Insight Study Guide series

Copyright © 20011 Insight Publications Pty Ltd

First published in 2009 by
Insight Publications Pty Ltd
ABN 57 005 102 983
89 Wellington Street
St Kilda VIC 3182
Australia
Tel: +61 3 9523 0044
Fax: +61 3 9523 2044
Email: books@insightpublications.com
Website: www.insightpublications.com

This edition published 2011 in the United States of America by
Insight Publications Pty Ltd, Australia.

ISBN-13: 978-1-921411-41-0

All rights reserved. Except as permitted under U.S. Copyright Act of 1976,
no part of this publication may be reproduced, distributed, or transmitted in any
form or by any means, or stored in a database or retrieval system, without the
prior written permission of the publisher.

Library of Congress Control Number: 2011931347

Cover Design by The Modern Art Production Group
Cover Illustrations by The Modern Art Production Group,
istockphoto® and House Industries
Internal Design by Sarn Potter

Printed in the United States of America by Lightning Source
10 9 8 7 6 5 4 3 2 1

contents

CHARACTER MAP

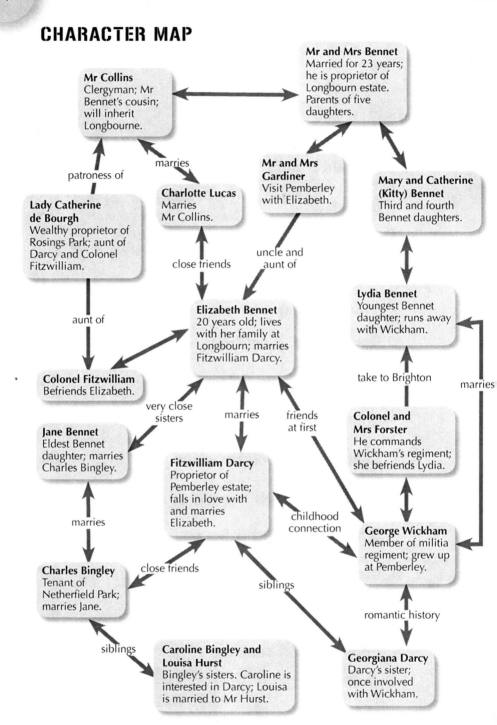

OVERVIEW

About the author

Jane Austen was born on 16 December 1775 in the village of Steventon in the English county of Hampshire, and was seventh of the eight children of George and Cassandra (nee Leigh). George was rector of the Steventon parish and he and Cassandra also ran a small school for boys of the neighbourhood. The Austen parents were very interested in literature and learning, and Cassandra wrote poetry.

Austen spent some years at boarding school but was predominantly educated at home. She began writing as a child and by her early twenties had completed draft versions of her novels *Sense and Sensibility* and *Pride and Prejudice*. In 1801 George Austen retired and Jane, along with her parents and elder sister (also named Cassandra) relocated to the resort town of Bath. The move was ostensibly to take advantage of the easier lifestyle and healthier environment of Bath but may also have been designed to enhance the daughters' marriage opportunities. By this point, Austen had already experienced romantic disappointment. Around 1795 she seems to have fallen in love with a young Irishman named Tom Lefroy and to have had her feelings reciprocated. It was not considered a financially advantageous match, however, as Tom was obliged to enter a career in the law in order to support his family and Jane had no fortune to bring to a marriage. Living in Bath did not bring her into contact with any serious suitors, although in 1802 she initially accepted and then rejected a proposal from a family friend, Harris Bigg-Wither. Her actions in relation to this offer have been interpreted as a rejection of marrying for security or material comfort (Irvine 2005, p.3). Ultimately, Austen's closest relationship would be with her sister Cassandra, who also remained unmarried following the death of her fiancé.

In 1805 George Austen died and his estate passed to his eldest son James; the Austen women were now dependent on their male relatives for support and were obliged to move in with James and his family. In 1809 they were offered the opportunity to live independently in a cottage in the village of Chawton in their home county of Hampshire. Austen had sold her first novel, *Susan* (later published as *Northanger*

Abbey), in Bath but devoted herself more intensely to writing following the attainment of a secure base in Chawton. It was here that she revised and published *Sense and Sensibility* (1811) and *Pride and Prejudice* (1813), and that she wrote *Mansfield Park* (1814), *Emma* (1815) and *Persuasion* (published posthumously in 1817). Austen was at work on another novel, *Sanditon*, when she fell ill in 1816. Jane Austen died on 18 July 1817 at the age of 41.

Synopsis

The Bennet family's settled existence in the village of Meryton is disrupted by the arrival of Charles Bingley and his sisters at nearby Netherfield Park. A series of social events brings together Bingley and the eldest Bennet daughter, Jane, and the engagement of the two seems increasingly likely. The Bennet family also becomes acquainted with Bingley's friend, the rich and imperious Fitzwilliam Darcy, who quickly makes himself disagreeable to the neighbourhood. The second Bennet daughter, Elizabeth, expresses a particular dislike for Darcy. The Bennet family is further unsettled by the sudden appearance of Mr Bennet's cousin, Mr Collins, who stands to inherit the family estate. Having been encouraged by his patroness, Lady Catherine de Bourgh, to find a wife, he proposes to Elizabeth and is rejected, to the considerable anger and annoyance of Mrs Bennet. Mr Collins promptly transfers his attentions to Elizabeth's friend, Charlotte Lucas, who does accept his offer of marriage.

The youngest Bennet daughters, Catherine (Kitty) and Lydia, are excited by the arrival of a militia regiment in the neighbourhood and the family quickly befriends many of the officers, including the charming and gregarious George Wickham. Wickham, the son of the elder Mr Darcy's steward, tells Elizabeth of his mistreatment at the hands of the younger Mr Darcy, information that strengthens her animosity towards Darcy. Meanwhile, Jane's hopes for marriage to Bingley are compromised by his return to London and by his sisters' cool behaviour towards her. Bingley's own inattention seems to confirm his disinterest.

Elizabeth visits Charlotte at her new home and is introduced to Lady Catherine. Darcy and his cousin, Colonel Fitzwilliam, arrive to visit their aunt at this time. The Colonel informs Elizabeth of Darcy's recent intervention in a friend's relationship with a young woman, a connection. Darcy had considered unsuitable. Elizabeth assumes the Colonel is referring to Bingley and Jane and is incensed. When Darcy subsequently proposes to her, his arrogant demeanour and her understanding of his role in Wickham's and Jane's affairs prompts a spirited refusal. Darcy writes to Elizabeth, refuting Wickham's claims and declaring he influenced Bingley because he believed Jane's cool attitude was indicative of a lack of real feeling on her part. Further reports of Wickham's behaviour and closer acquaintance with Darcy following a visit to his estate force Elizabeth to reassess her initial impressions of both men.

Wickham's dissolute (immoral) nature is later confirmed when the family receives news of his and Lydia's departure from Brighton. They are pursued by Elizabeth's uncle, Mr Gardiner, and forced to marry and salvage the Bennet family's reputation. Elizabeth later learns that Darcy was instrumental in achieving this resolution – news that further complicates her feelings for him. Bingley meanwhile has returned to Netherfield Park; he resolves issues with Jane and they are engaged, to the delight of the whole family. The subsequent revelation of Elizabeth and Darcy's engagement produces emotions that are more mixed, from Mr Bennet's incredulity to Lady Catherine's outrage. The couple remain resolute and their happy future is assured.

Character summaries

Mr Bennet

Patriarch of the Bennet family. He belongs to the minor gentry, deriving a relatively small income from the land attached to his estate. Very fond of Elizabeth. As Mr Bennet has no sons, the inheritance of the estate will pass to Mr Collins.

Mrs Bennet

Mr Bennet's wife of 23 years. Her principal object in life is to find husbands for her five daughters. Dotes on Lydia and is less fond of Elizabeth.

Jane Bennet

The eldest Bennet daughter. She is particularly close to Elizabeth and they share each other's confidences. Befriended by the Bingley sisters and ultimately marries their brother Charles. Known for her beauty and good nature.

Elizabeth Bennet

Twenty years old; the second-eldest of the Bennet sisters. A bright and independent woman. She is her father's favourite and her mother's least favourite daughter. Marries Fitzwilliam Darcy.

Mary Bennet

The third daughter; considered the 'intellectual' of the family. She busies herself with reading and music.

Catherine (Kitty) Bennet

The fourth daughter; 18 years old. She is particularly close to Lydia and shares her enthusiasm for amusements.

Lydia Bennet

The youngest Bennet daughter; 15 years old. Has much in common with Mrs Bennet and is her mother's particular favourite. Very prone to flirting, especially with the officers in Meryton. She runs away with, and eventually marries, George Wickham.

Fitzwilliam Darcy

Twenty-eight years old; the owner of the magnificent country estate, Pemberley. Has an income of 10,000 pounds a year, but a reputation as a proud and ill-mannered man. Close friend of Charles Bingley and potential suitor of Caroline Bingley and Anne de Bourgh. He falls in love with, and marries, Elizabeth Bennet.

Charles Bingley

Inherits the fortune his father built through manufacturing and trade interests; leases Netherfield Park with a view to establishing his own country estate. He falls in love with Jane and, despite objections of his family and close friend Darcy, succeeds in marrying her.

Caroline Bingley and Louisa Hurst

Charles Bingley's sisters; each command a fortune of 20,000 pounds. They join him at Netherfield, although their principal residence remains in London. Louisa is married to Mr Hurst. Caroline endeavours, unsuccessfully, to attract the romantic interest of Darcy.

Charlotte Lucas

Twenty-seven years old; the eldest child of Sir William and Lady Lucas; Elizabeth's closest friend. She marries Mr Collins and moves to Hunsford parsonage.

Sir William Lucas and Maria Lucas

Sir William's role as former mayor of Meryton led to his being knighted by George III. His daughter Maria shares her father's awe for titles and status.

Mr Collins

Twenty-five years old; Mr Bennet's cousin. The Bennets' closest male relative; according to the laws of entail, stands to inherit Longbourn. A clergyman, he has recently secured the living of Hunsford parsonage. Under the patronage of Lady Catherine de Bourgh; shows excessive gratitude to her. Marries Charlotte Lucas.

Mr Wickham

A member of the militia regiment posted to Meryton. He is the son of the late Mr Darcy's steward and has known Fitzwilliam Darcy since childhood. He marries Lydia and accepts a station in the north of the country.

Lady Catherine de Bourgh and Anne de Bourgh

A wealthy widow of high social standing, Lady Catherine lives with her daughter Anne at Rosings Park. She is the sister of Darcy's late mother and intends for him to marry Anne.

Mr and Mrs Gardiner

Mr Gardiner, Mrs Bennet's brother, is a businessman in trade in London. He and his wife have four small children. Mrs Gardiner is particularly close to Jane and Elizabeth; she often acts as Elizabeth's confidante.

Colonel Fitzwilliam

Darcy's cousin. Accompanies the latter on a visit to their aunt, Lady Catherine; develops a friendship with Elizabeth.

Georgiana Darcy

Sixteen years old; Darcy's sister. It is rumoured that she is due to marry Charles Bingley. Was previously involved with Wickham.

Colonel and Mrs Forster

Colonel Forster commands the militia regiment stationed in Meryton. His wife becomes a close friend of Lydia; invites her to join them when the militia relocates to Brighton.

Mrs Reynolds

Housekeeper at Pemberley. Has known Darcy since he was a child; has a high opinion of him.

Note on page references

Throughout this text guide we have provided page references to the two editions of *Pride and Prejudice* published by Penguin: the 'Black Classics' edition (with the black strip across the bottom of the front cover, 2003), and the 'Red Classics' edition (2006). Page numbers are given as B and R respectively.

BACKGROUND & CONTEXT

Social hierarchy

When Austen's niece Anna ventured into writing, the novelist commented on a manuscript the latter sent her to critique: '3 or 4 families in a Country Village is the very thing to work on … You are but *now* coming to the heart and beauty of your book' (Kelly 1989, p.116). Austen discovered a rich seam of material in the dynamics of families and small communities. Yet even within this limited perspective, *Pride and Prejudice* offers significant insight into the shifting social strata (layers) of late 18th-century society.

Austen was born into a society undergoing immense change yet still defined by a strict hierarchy which was largely determined by economic power. At the top of the hierarchy were the aristocracy, whose status was based on inherited wealth. The landed gentry existed on a social plane below the aristocracy. Their wealth was also inherited but based on property ownership; they lived on the interest generated by their capital. The aristocracy and gentry formed the power base of the old social order, and in Austen's time their power was beginning to be challenged. The growth of a capitalist system (an economic model based on private rather than state ownership of commerce and industry) in the wake of the

Industrial Revolution strengthened the middle classes, whose means of generating income were based on trade and commerce. The rise of the middle classes broadened access to economic power and threatened to destabilise traditional class boundaries.

Jane Austen's own social standing is a useful example in forming a context for the representations of class in her novels:

> an understanding of precisely where one stood in the social hierarchy was important to anyone in England in this period: the Austens stood below gentry families ... but, because George was university-educated, above any kind of merchant ... (Irvine 2005, p.6)

Irvine makes the point that social advancement in this world was determined by familial and neighbourhood connections with people of greater status: a system known as patronage. In *Pride and Prejudice*, Wickham claims to have secured the patronage of Darcy's father and Mr Collins has been made the rector of Hunsford parsonage under the patronage of Lady Catherine.

The novel contains families and individuals representing a range of class positions. At the top of the social hierarchy, due to their economic capital and aristocratic connections, are Darcy and Lady Catherine. With an income based on manufacturing interests, the Bingleys are less socially secure and yet their wealth affords them considerable status. The Bennet family is reasonably comfortable – they are able, for example, to maintain a number of household staff – but the daughters have little personal fortune and the only way they can really hope to improve their social situation is through marriage. *Pride and Prejudice* also incorporates a portrait of the rising middle classes in its depiction of the Gardiners, who derive their income from a profession. The middle classes were often treated with disdain and suspicion by the gentry; Elizabeth demonstrates her consciousness of such prejudice in her reactions to Darcy's opinion of the Gardiners before he meets them.

Politics and revolution

Jane Austen has been critiqued for the 'insularity' of her work and its lack of engagement with the wider world:

> ... during a decade in which Napoleon was effectively engaging, if not transforming, Europe, Jane Austen composed a novel in which the most important events are the fact that a man changes his manners and a young lady changes her mind ... (Tanner 1986, p.103)

Austen lived during a period of significant political instability. Despite her relatively sheltered home environment, she would have been acutely aware of developments in the wider world, including the French Revolution and the ongoing conflicts with France. Such events impacted personally on her family: two of her brothers were in the navy, and her cousin Eliza's French husband was guillotined during the Reign of Terror (a period of mass executions orchestrated by the revolutionaries) in Paris.

Pride and Prejudice makes some reference to contemporary events and critics have used these to help identify the chronological setting of the novel. Based on the movements of the militia regiment, Robert Irvine sets the events of the novel in 1793–94 or 1794–95 (Irvine 2005, p.56). England was at war with France from 1793; in response to this threat, militia regiments such as the one depicted in *Pride and Prejudice* were mobilised for action. A more precise historical reference is included in Chapter 61. The narrator comments on Wickham and Lydia's fortunes following the 'restoration of peace' and Wickham's subsequent demobilisation from the forces (p.366B; p.426R). In her notes to the text, Vivien Jones notes this 'might refer to the temporary cessation of hostilities with France at the Treaty of Amiens of March 1802' (p.435B).

The female sphere

Women of the aristocracy and gentry were generally separated from the world of work and commerce. The placement of women within a separate 'sphere' began in childhood: girls typically received a more limited education than their brothers. In Chapter 29 Elizabeth tells Lady Catherine that she and her sisters have been largely self-taught, with teachers brought in for certain areas. Girls were encouraged to focus less on learning than on the acquisition of 'accomplishments' such as music, drawing and embroidery. In Chapter 8 Darcy and Caroline express their views on female accomplishments. According to the latter, a 'woman must have a thorough knowledge of music, singing, drawing, dancing and the modern languages' (p.39B; p.43R). Elizabeth's challenges to their exacting standards are evidence of her individuality.

Women were subjected to stricter standards of behaviour than their male counterparts. They were supposed to be modest, retiring and self-effacing; in *Pride and Prejudice*, Jane is presented as a model of female decorum. Part of the reason Elizabeth captures Darcy's interest is her uncommon spirit and willingness to air her opinions – aspects of character that draw the Bingley sisters' criticisms. Elizabeth's behaviour remains within the bounds of propriety, however, unlike Lydia's. The youngest Bennet's boisterous, flirtatious manner leaves her open to criticism even before she has committed the far more serious transgression of running away with Wickham.

Publishing context

Pride and Prejudice's earliest incarnation was as a story titled 'First Impressions' which Austen completed in 1796. A year later, Austen's father sent the manuscript to a London publisher but it was rejected. The novel was finally published anonymously, under the title *Pride and Prejudice*, in 1813. No versions survive to suggest how the novel developed in the intervening period, but it certainly underwent revision, as Austen herself stated she had 'lop't and crop't' it (Tomalin 1997, p.154).

There was considerable precedent for Austen – a woman – to pursue a writing career at this time. Increasing numbers of popular and critically acclaimed female writers were emerging, working not just with the novel form but also with poetry, drama, essays and journalism. Yet obstacles remained to prevent women from entering the public sphere in this way. For example, women were not allowed to make legal arrangements independently. So it was necessary to have a male agent act on behalf of a female writer and liaise with a publisher. Those women who did achieve publication also faced considerable prejudice and many felt forced to publish anonymously or under an assumed name. It is popularly believed that only Austen's immediate family knew of her work. However, this claim has been rejected by recent biographers, who suggest her identity as an author was known by many people, including the Prince of Wales – who was such a fan of her work that he informed her she could dedicate her novel *Emma* to him.

GENRE, STRUCTURE & LANGUAGE

The novel and narrative point of view

Novels can be defined broadly as fictional prose narratives. The novel gained prominence as a form in the 18th century. Austen works within the form of the **realist novel**. In contrast to other genres such as romance or gothic, the realist novel distinguishes itself by its focus on recognisable characters and events. The realist novel is characterised by a commitment to **verisimilitude**, or an accurate description of the surrounding world.

Many early novels were in **epistolary** form, meaning the narrative consisted of a series of letters sent between the characters. As a first-person narrative, the epistolary novel allows the inner thoughts and feelings of a character to be easily communicated to the reader. However, it is less suited to building a sense of context – of the world the characters inhabit. This requires a form that suggests distance and objectivity, such as the **omniscient third-person** narrative. In this form the narrator sits over and above the text, describing events to the reader. Critics suggest Austen adopted a style that allowed her to combine the personal insight of a first-person narrative with the objectivity of a third-person narrative. This style is known as **free indirect discourse**. In free indirect discourse the text is ostensibly narrated in the third person but at times seems to reflect the point of view of a particular character. This allows the author to communicate the characters' inner thoughts and feelings *and* to comment, more or less objectively, on the context of the narrative.

There are also some interesting moments in the novel where we hear what appears to be the voice of the narrator speaking directly to the reader. One example of this occurs in Chapter 26, where Mrs Gardiner advises Elizabeth to be cautious in her dealings with Wickham, due to his lack of fortune. The narrator describes this as 'a wonderful instance of advice being given on such a point, without being resented' (p.143B; p.164R).

The novel makes extensive use of **dialogue**, which is the reported speech of the characters. Dialogue reveals how the characters relate to one another, thus it is through dialogue that we gain a sense of Mrs Bennet's dislike of Darcy. We also hear the voice of the character through dialogue and build a sense of his or her personality. Our understanding of Lydia, for example, is developed through her ecstatic responses to various events. Depending on the context, dialogue can introduce us to both the public and private voices of the characters.

A more intimate form of first-person narration is incorporated into the text through the use of letters written from one character to another. Letters are used to report on events and, more importantly, to convey emotions and interpretations. The most important letter in *Pride and Prejudice* is Darcy's to Elizabeth in Chapter 35, as it represents the first real challenge to her understanding of his character.

Comedy

Pride and Prejudice can be classified as **comedy** and the novel employs a range of narrative techniques to build humour. We see, for example, the development of comedy through characterisation. Mrs Bennet's foolishness, Mr Collins' obsequiousness and Lady Catherine's hauteur all become sources of humour. In Chapter 25 Mrs Bennet laments to Mrs Gardiner over Elizabeth's refusal of Mr Collins to the benefit of Charlotte Lucas:

> It makes me very nervous and poorly, to be thwarted so in my own family, and to have neighbours who think of themselves before anybody else. However, your coming just at this time is the greatest of comforts, and I am very glad to hear what you tell us, of long sleeves … (p.138B; p.159R)

The representation of Mrs Bennet shows how some of the humour in the novel takes on the darker edge of **satire**. Satire is the use of comic techniques to ridicule a folly or vice. Mrs Bennet's excessive emotion, and rapid shift from a focus on personal slights to an interest in details of fashion, exposes her shallow nature and renders her ridiculous.

Elizabeth herself becomes the source of comedy at the opening of Chapter 33, as she fails to read the significance of her repeated meetings with Darcy while out walking, even though she has expressly informed him of the route of her morning walk so that he might avoid her. These meetings demonstrate his obvious desire for her company, and the narrative invites us to laugh at her expense.

Structure

Austen uses a three-volume structure for *Pride and Prejudice*. There are 23 chapters in Volume One; 19 in Volume Two; and 19 in Volume Three. The central focus within the novel is the Bennet family; the central figure – or protagonist – is the second-eldest daughter, Elizabeth. The relationship between Elizabeth and Darcy forms the core of the narrative. This plotline engages our attention at the beginning of the novel and is only satisfactorily resolved in the final chapters. The relationships of Jane and Bingley; Charlotte and Mr Collins; and Lydia and Wickham form the principal subplots.

Whilst much of the action is centred on the Bennet family estate (Longbourn) and their home village of Meryton, each volume also includes episodes that take Elizabeth further afield and expose her to a wider social circle. In Volume One, Jane's illness forces Elizabeth to spend several days at Netherfield Park; in Volume Two she visits Hunsford parsonage and Rosings Park; and in Volume Three she is taken to Pemberley. Each of these experiences represents an increasing challenge to her earlier perceptions of Darcy and of her own family situation.

Several features of *Pride and Prejudice*'s structure help build suspense. One example is the use of **foreshadowing**. Foreshadowing is the arrangement of the narrative to suggest future developments. In Chapter 21 Caroline Bingley's letter to Jane is the principal focus; however, the narrative makes subtle references to other plotlines, namely Mr Collins' spending time with Charlotte, and Elizabeth's growing affinity with Wickham and agreement with him on the subject of Darcy. This arrangement of detail demonstrates Austen's technique of foreshadowing events; she provides the reader with clues and insights and allows them to foresee possible developments.

Irony

In Austen's novels, the mode of expression and the tone of the narrative voice are very important and need to be examined closely. In free indirect discourse, the narrative moves between the third-person voice of the narrator and the voices of individual characters. This can create **irony**, an important feature of Austen's writing. Irony occurs when there is a discrepancy between what is *said* and what is *implied*. The opening sentence of *Pride and Prejudice* is a famous example of Austen's use of irony: 'It is a truth universally acknowledged, that a single man in possession of a good fortune, must be in want of a wife' (p.5B; p.3R). Whilst the surface meaning is that wealthy men desire wives, the implied meaning is that single women are looking for rich husbands.

CHAPTER-BY-CHAPTER ANALYSIS

Note: in the **Key Vocabulary** sections I have only provided definitions for words and phrases not included in Vivien Jones' notes to the 2003 Penguin Classics edition.

Volume One Chapter 1

Summary: *The Bennet family discusses the arrival of Mr Bingley to the neighbourhood.*

In Chapter 1, the reader is given an insight into the conventions of the world depicted in *Pride and Prejudice*. We learn that Mrs Bennet and her daughters should not visit Mr Bingley before *Mr* Bennet has called on him. This chapter also establishes certain family dynamics, notably Mr Bennet's favouritism for Lizzy among his daughters.

Key vocabulary
Establishment: household.
Quickness: alertness.
Develope: uncover.
Mean: narrow.

Q Does Mr Bennet's preference for Lizzy invite the reader to value her more highly than the other Bennet girls?

Chapter 2

Summary: *Mr Bennet informs his family of his visit to Mr Bingley.*

The issue of an introduction to Mr Bingley is the basis for comedy in this chapter, which opens by informing the reader that Mr Bennet *has* made the visit. Yet he allows Mrs Bennet to continue in the assumption that he is refusing to go. The chapter deepens our understanding of the Bennet family dynamics, particularly between the parents.

Key vocabulary
Waited on: visited.

Q How would you characterise the relationship between Mr and Mrs Bennet?

Chapter 3

Summary: *The ball at the assembly rooms; introduction of Mr Bingley and Mr Darcy.*

The ball scene suggests that, whilst money is very well regarded in this society, so is temperament and personality. Unlike Bingley, Darcy seems unwilling to dance with the families of the neighbourhood and congregates only with Miss Bingley and Mrs Hurst. His attitude could be interpreted as shyness but is instead read as pride and pomposity: 'His character was decided. He was the proudest, most disagreeable man in the world, and every body hoped that he would never come there again' (p.13B; p.11R). The community's attitude to Darcy provides a striking early example of the workings of 'first impressions'.

Key vocabulary
Noble mein: noble bearing or demeanour.
Principal inhabitants: individuals of the highest status in the village, as determined by class or wealth.

Chapter 4

Summary: *Elizabeth and Jane share their confidences; background information is given about the Bingley family and Mr Darcy.*

This chapter offers our first intimate encounter with Elizabeth and Jane and establishes the importance of their sisterly relationship. It also suggests their status as judges of character. Jane sees only the good in people and is perhaps blinkered to their true attitudes and motivations. Elizabeth appears more discerning in her judgements, particularly of the Bingley sisters.

Key vocabulary
Ductility: malleability.

Chapter 5

Summary: *Introduction of the Lucas family.*

In this chapter the Lucas daughters visit the Bennets to talk over the assembly ball. Bingley's partiality for Jane is discussed, as is Darcy's behaviour. The general opinion of the latter is negative, although Jane and Charlotte offer more moderate views. Jane's comments suggest she believes he is shy, whilst Charlotte attributes his behaviour to his class position.

Chapter 6

Summary: *Elizabeth and Charlotte discuss Jane's feelings for Mr Bingley; Elizabeth declines to dance with Mr Darcy.*

Charlotte believes Jane is too reserved around Bingley and addresses the danger of a woman not offering a potential suitor enough encouragement. Charlotte is a pragmatist and frames the building of a relationship strategically: Jane should not 'allow' herself to fall in love until she is 'secure' in Bingley's attachment and has received a definite proposal of marriage (p.23B; p.24R). Elizabeth, in contrast, believes the compatibility of the couple should be paramount. This difference of approach will be borne out in the friends' respective marriages.

Q How are the issues Charlotte and Elizabeth raise reflected in the development of Jane and Bingley's relationship?

Chapter 7

Summary: *There's news of a military regiment being stationed at Meryton; Jane is forced by an illness to spend the night at Netherfield; Elizabeth goes to keep Jane company.*

Mrs Bennet's dedication to devising strategies that will foster opportunities for courtship is demonstrated by her attitude to Jane's transport to Netherfield. Jane would rather travel by coach as it is more elegant and offers protection from the weather. However, the horses are also needed for agricultural work and Mrs Bennet uses this fact to force Jane to walk. The older woman's indifferent attitude to her daughter's comfort and wishes is strikingly drawn. Mr Bennet suggests his wife overlooks the horses' agricultural purpose when it suits her to do so, to which

Elizabeth adds: 'But if you have got them to day … my mother's purpose will be answered' (p.31B; p.34R). This comment forces the decision on Mr Bennet. Perhaps Elizabeth is offering him an opportunity to override his wife's scheming – an opportunity he fails to take up.

Q What do the responses of the Netherfield party to Elizabeth's sudden arrival suggest about an understanding of 'proper' female behaviour?

Chapter 8

Summary: Jane and Elizabeth continue their stay at Netherfield.

Jane's illness offers Elizabeth insight into life at Netherfield, and the opportunity to study its inhabitants and their relationships. Meanwhile, the presence of the Bennet sisters provides the Bingley sisters with further opportunities to express disdain for the country girls' lifestyle, customs and relations. Whilst Bingley is unconcerned by their family connections, Darcy takes a more cynical view, suggesting such relations 'must very materially lessen their chance of marrying men of any consideration in the world' (p.37B; p.40R).

Chapter 9

Summary: Mrs Bennet, Lydia and Catherine visit Netherfield.

Mrs Bennet continues to exploit Jane's illness to further the latter's relationship with Mr Bingley. Yet Mrs Bennet's behaviour on this occasion, including several slights at Darcy, only causes embarrassment, of which she herself is completely unaware. Lydia's gauche reminders about the promised ball at Netherfield also demonstrate the distance between certain female members of the Bennet family and the refined Bingley sisters.

Q What does the debate about city versus country life (pp.42–3B; pp.46–8R) reveal about the characters' personalities and attitudes?

Chapter 10

Summary: Elizabeth observes Caroline's efforts to charm Darcy; Elizabeth and Darcy discuss the nature of friendship.

In this chapter, comparisons are drawn between Darcy and Bingley as letter-writers: comparisons that are suggestive of their differences in personality. Bingley claims Darcy writes wordy, painstakingly studied letters, whilst admitting his own are more impulsive as his 'ideas flow so rapidly' (p.47B; p.52R). It is these differences (Bingley's impulsivity and Darcy's caution) that will mark the direction of their romantic relationships.

KEY POINT

This chapter makes explicit Darcy's growing admiration for Elizabeth – his delight in her beauty, intelligence and charm. Yet his awareness of her inferior social position acts as a check on his feelings and, as a result, Elizabeth continues to read his admiration as critique.

Key vocabulary

Panegyric: praise.

Q How does this chapter suggest Caroline's awareness of the threat Elizabeth poses?

Chapter 11

Summary: *Jane joins the Netherfield party after dinner; Caroline invites Elizabeth to parade around the room with her.*

This is a useful chapter for detailed analysis of the characterisation of Elizabeth and Darcy, and the nature of their interaction. Whilst Elizabeth values openness and an ability to laugh at the foibles of oneself and others, Darcy abhors any signs of weakness and the ridicule they provoke. He is a highly guarded individual, and easily offended.

Q When Darcy tells Elizabeth that 'where there is a real superiority of mind, pride will be always under good regulation', she turns 'away to hide a smile' (p.56B; p.62R). How do you read the meaning of her action here?

Chapter 12

Summary: *Darcy decides to avoid Elizabeth; Jane and Elizabeth return home.*

This chapter charts the Bennet sisters' departure from Netherfield and the responses it elicits. These include Mrs Bennet's efforts to have them remain at Netherfield; Mr Bingley's disappointment at Jane's departure;

Elizabeth's longing to return home; and Darcy's mixed feelings. Darcy expresses concern that Elizabeth might be encouraged by his behaviour and resolves to act more coolly towards her.

Chapter 13

Summary: *Mr Bennet shares Mr Collins' letter with the family; Collins arrives.*

In this chapter we learn more of the economic position of the Bennet daughters, namely that on their father's death his estate will pass to his cousin Mr Collins. This puts the daughters in a precarious position and fuels Mrs Bennet's efforts to have them swiftly married. The entailment is a sore point with Mrs Bennet, as she does not understand its legal basis and responds to it only with emotion.

Q What does Elizabeth's response to Mr Collins' letter reveal about her ability to be a good judge of character?

Key Point

Pride and Prejudice reflects women's status as second-class citizens in the eyes of the law and in customs of inheritance. Key aspects of the plot result from the 'entail' on the Bennet estate. The Bennet entail does not allow for a daughter to inherit, therefore the estate will pass to Mr Collins as the closest male relative.

Chapter 14

Summary: *The Bennet family becomes acquainted with Mr Collins.*

Mr Collins possesses a strict moral code, as revealed in his reaction to the presence of a novel from a circulating library in the Bennet household. He expresses a conservative response to the novel as an improper influence, particularly on young women. His attitude is emphasised when he selects instead the Reverend James Fordyce's *Sermons to Young Women* to read aloud: a text that exhorts the evils of novel-reading. This incident not only gives us an insight into Mr Collins' character but also suggests the relatively liberal environment in which Kitty and Lydia have been raised.

Chapter 15

Summary: *Mr Collins' marriage plans are revealed; Mr Wickham is introduced.*

Mr Collins' plan to marry one of the Bennet daughters is framed as a magnanimous (generous) gesture – a means of making amends for his inheritance of the Bennet estate. He goes so far as to consider his own intentions 'excessively generous' (p.69B; p.78R). His rapid switch of focus from Jane to Elizabeth – upon being informed by Mrs Bennet that the former may already have secured the interest of another – demonstrates that he intends a strategic, rather than a romantic, alliance.

Q Why does Mrs Bennet seem so willing to support Mr Collins' plans to marry one of her daughters?

Chapter 16

Summary: *Wickham tells Elizabeth of his history with Darcy.*

Elizabeth's strenuous assertion of her dislike for Darcy encourages Wickham in his stories of the latter's slights towards him. Wickham is an expert manipulator and frames his story in terms that encourage Elizabeth's belief. He claims his warm relationship with Darcy's father was the catalyst for the son's dislike and subsequent actions, implying that Darcy was jealous of him. He cleverly builds on Elizabeth's reference to Darcy's 'pride' (p.80B; p.91R). Wickham uses her own prejudices to help persuade Elizabeth that the good deeds she's heard Darcy has committed were also motivated by pride.

Q Why does Elizabeth form such an immediate attachment to Wickham?

Chapter 17

Summary: *Jane and Elizabeth discuss the implications of Wickham's story; Mr Bingley and his sisters visit Longbourn with invitations to a ball.*

The Bingley sisters' preference for Jane is again evident in this chapter, as they virtually disregard all other members of the Bennet family on their visit to Longbourn. Elizabeth's interest in Wickham is confirmed when she views the ball as an opportunity to enjoy his company. Her enthusiasm for the ball backfires, however, when she finds herself engaged in advance for the first two dances with Mr Collins. This action indicates his intentions towards her, as Elizabeth herself soon realises.

Q How do the Bennet women's different responses to the invitation (p.85B; p.96R) advance our understanding of their individual personalities?

Chapter 18

Summary: *The Netherfield ball; Elizabeth dances with Darcy; Caroline challenges Wickham's story; Jane's engagement to Bingley seems assured.*

The opening paragraph demonstrates the extent to which Elizabeth has warmed to Wickham. She tells Charlotte she is now 'determined to hate' Darcy as Wickham's enemy (p.89B; p.101R). Her strategy of avoidance is foiled when Darcy surprises her with an invitation to dance, which she uses as an opportunity to test Wickham's claims. Darcy quickly recognises Wickham's influence in Elizabeth's questions.

Q Why does Elizabeth attempt to prevent Mr Collins from introducing himself to Darcy?

Chapter 19

Summary: *Mr Collins proposes to Elizabeth.*

Austen's comic sensibility is on display in the scene of Mr Collins' proposal to Elizabeth. His pompous assurances that she will be honoured by his offer are undercut throughout by her discomfort with the situation and her distaste for him. His inability to accept her rejection becomes almost farcical as he persists in interpreting her refusal as an example of feminine wiles or excessive modesty. Less amusing is Mrs Bennet's wilful disregard for her daughter's wishes. She actively encourages Mr Collins with scant concern for Elizabeth's own desires or for the suitability of the match.

Chapter 20

Summary: *Mrs Bennet coaxes Elizabeth to accept Mr Collins' offer.*

The disparate interests and perspectives of the Bennet parents are further evidenced in this chapter, with their responses to Mr Collins' proposal to

Elizabeth. Mr Bennet quickly and quietly sides with his daughter before retreating back into the sanctuary of the library. Mrs Bennet, in contrast, cajoles, chastises and harangues Elizabeth to accept the offer.

Q Consider Mrs Bennet's long speech (p.111B; p.126R). What are her motives for wanting Elizabeth to marry Mr Collins?

Chapter 21

Summary: *Mr Collins turns his attentions to Charlotte Lucas; Jane receives a letter from Caroline Bingley.*

Caroline's letter to Jane represents the first complication in the latter's burgeoning relationship with Charles. Caroline attempts to sabotage the relationship by telling Jane she is unlikely to enjoy further contact with Charles as he plans to remain in town; furthermore, she suggests he is involved with Georgiana Darcy and Caroline anticipates their engagement. Whilst Jane trusts the truth of Caroline's claims, Elizabeth is more astute and challenges her sister's straightforward reading of the letter. She identifies Caroline's class anxiety about a possible marriage between Jane and Charles, and suggests that the attempt to unite Charles and Georgiana stems from Caroline's own desire to marry Darcy.

Chapter 22

Summary: *Mr Collins is engaged to Charlotte Lucas.*

Events in this chapter demonstrate the relationship between marriage and status for women in this society. Charlotte would rather marry a man she does not love and thus become mistress of her own house than remain in the position of unmarried daughter, dependent on her parents or siblings. Interestingly, Austen does not redeem Mr Collins in any way; the narrative emphasises his unattractive qualities, such as 'stupidity' (p.120B; p.137R) and lack of humour. In the eyes of Charlotte and her parents these factors are outweighed by his ability to provide for a wife.

Chapter 23

Summary: *Charlotte's engagement to Mr Collins is announced.*

The first volume of the novel closes with Mrs Bennet's chagrin (embarrassment and irritation) at Charlotte's engagement and at the reports that Mr Bingley will not be returning to Netherfield. Her two eldest daughters' engagements – of which she had previously felt so confident – have now been significantly compromised. Mrs Bennet's attitude lends a pessimistic air to the end of the volume: even Elizabeth is affected by it.

Volume Two Chapter 24

Summary: *Jane receives a second letter from Caroline; Elizabeth confides to Jane her feelings about Charlotte's engagement and Charles Bingley's behaviour.*

Elizabeth criticises Bingley's weakness in the face of Caroline's machinations (manipulations) and is angered by how his behaviour impacts on Jane. Jane is unable to believe the Bingley women could negatively influence their brother in his choice of wife. Rather, she suggests that if he had genuine feelings for her they would be *unable* to do so. Jane concludes that he therefore was not really attached to her and she had simply been indulging her own 'fancy' (p.134B; p.154R).

Q How valid do you consider Elizabeth's criticisms of Bingley?

Chapter 25

Summary: *Arrival of Mr and Mrs Gardiner; Jane is invited to return with them to London.*

The arrival of Mr and Mrs Gardiner allows various plot points to be developed. Mrs Gardiner has previously lived in Derbyshire, the home county of both Darcy and Wickham. She is able to confirm Wickham's impressions of Pemberley and his statements regarding the good nature of Darcy's father. She further supports Wickham's cause by uncovering a dim recollection of 'Mr Fitzwilliam Darcy formerly spoken of as a very proud, ill-natured boy' (p.141B; p.162R).

Chapter 26

Summary: *Mrs Gardiner cautions Elizabeth about marriage to Wickham; Mr Collins and Charlotte are married; Jane writes to Elizabeth of visiting Caroline in London; Elizabeth writes to her aunt with news of Wickham's attachment to a Miss King.*

Mrs Gardiner warns Elizabeth against marriage to Wickham not on the grounds of character but due to his lack of fortune. Elizabeth is not sure she could allow her head to govern her heart so wholly, recognising that she is vulnerable to 'temptation' (p.143B; p.164R). However, she promises her aunt she will exercise caution and not actively wish for, or encourage, an attachment.

Of further significance in this chapter is Jane's letter to Elizabeth, in which she writes of her changed opinion of Caroline Bingley. She is confused by Caroline's coolness towards her, especially as she is now certain it cannot arise from any anxiety about an attachment between herself and Charles.

Q Do you believe Elizabeth's claims that she has not been significantly troubled by the news of Wickham's new relationship?

Chapter 27

Summary: *Elizabeth spends a night in London with Jane and the Gardiners en route to visit Charlotte.*

Conversation between Elizabeth and Mrs Gardiner in this chapter generates the impression that Jane continues to hold feelings for Bingley. The discussion also confirms Elizabeth's acceptance of the situation with Wickham. The two women enjoy a spirited discussion about Wickham's intentions to choose a wife with money.

Chapter 28

Summary: *Elizabeth arrives at Hunsford parsonage and is invited to dinner at Rosings.*

Elizabeth performs a careful examination of Charlotte's married life and is pleased to witness her friend's contentment in her situation, despite the fact that Mr Collins seems as annoying as ever. Elizabeth is also offered her first glimpse of Lady Catherine and her daughter Anne.

Chapter 29

Summary: *Elizabeth, Mr and Mrs Collins and William and Maria Lucas dine at Rosings.*

The dinner at Rosings exposes the class attitudes of the various characters. Mr Collins is able to fully indulge his habits of flattery whilst Sir William and Maria are cowed by the grandeur of the house. Elizabeth examines the surroundings and the inhabitants of Rosings more dispassionately.

She pronounces Lady Catherine supercilious and arrogant; a woman who is accustomed to being deferred to, which Elizabeth fails to do, thereby piquing the older lady's interest.

Q What does this chapter suggest about Elizabeth's attitude to traditional class distinctions in her society?

Chapter 30

Summary: *Darcy and Colonel Fitzwilliam arrive at Rosings.*

This chapter offers further detail of daily life for women of Elizabeth's class, portraying the daily round of genteel pursuits, walks and visiting. It underscores the importance and potential complexity of social interactions in this world – from Miss de Bourgh's passing the time of day with Charlotte during her carriage outings to Lady Catherine's dependence on her neighbours for card partners. These interactions are governed by etiquette and command respect, and Darcy's failure to observe these protocols marks him as an iconoclast (someone who wilfully resists traditional practices and conventions).

Q Darcy has been absent from the narrative for 11 chapters. What is the effect of delaying his re-appearance for so long?

Chapter 31

Summary: *Elizabeth and Charlotte spend an evening at Rosings with Colonel Fitzwilliam and Darcy.*

This chapter presents Elizabeth and Darcy's first sustained interaction for some time. Bolstered by Colonel Fitzwilliam's friendly attentions towards her, Elizabeth comments on Darcy's actions at the Netherfield ball – commentary that is both tease and critique. Darcy attempts to excuse his behaviour; he claims he is unable to make himself comfortable with strangers by engaging in small talk. Elizabeth, however, suggests such interaction is simply a matter of practice, using her own talent with the piano as an analogy.

Q What do Darcy's excuses suggest of his character? Is he a snob? Or merely shy?

Chapter 32

Summary: *Darcy calls at the parsonage, finding Elizabeth alone.*

Darcy's surprise visit to the parsonage encourages us to think more deeply about this character and his intentions. Intending to make a general call on the ladies of the house, he is unsettled by finding Elizabeth alone. However, the very fact of his visit is unusual, considering his status and previous unsociability. Both he and Elizabeth use the visit to further their own interests – she seeks information on Bingley's departure from Netherfield, and he tests her views on whether a married woman need live close to her family.

Chapter 33

Summary: *Elizabeth meets Darcy several times whilst out walking; Colonel Fitzwilliam tells Elizabeth of Darcy's intervention in Bingley's relationship.*

Elizabeth learns through Colonel Fitzwilliam that Darcy intervened to caution a friend against 'a most imprudent marriage' (p.181B; p.206R). From this she is led to surmise that it was not Caroline but Darcy who was the principal agent in sabotaging Jane and Bingley's relationship. The use of words such as 'ruined' and 'evil' (p.182B; pp.207–8R) in describing Elizabeth's response to this conclusion demonstrates the strength of her feeling over the matter. Darcy now seems utterly damned in her opinion, especially as she can see no reason for his objection to Jane beyond class prejudice and self-interest, which she describes as the 'worst kind of pride' (p.182B; p.208R).

Chapter 34

Summary: *Darcy proposes to Elizabeth – and is rejected.*

Darcy's proposal is strikingly unconventional. He declares that he has 'struggled' against his feelings and considers Elizabeth's familial connections beneath him (p.185B; p.210R). His sense of her inferiority frees Elizabeth from undue pity or compassion for his situation and she is inspired to respond with similar honesty. Darcy's startled response to Elizabeth's admission that she does not return his feelings prompts a frank exchange. She is able to level her charges against him, namely that he interfered in Bingley's relationship with Jane and that he deprived Wickham of his promised advantages.

Chapter 35

Summary: *Darcy's letter to Elizabeth.*

Darcy uses his letter to Elizabeth to answer her charges against him. He credits Jane herself as the reason for his intervening in her relationship with Bingley. He accuses Jane of failing to demonstrate appropriate sentiments towards his friend, and of instead remaining 'indifferent' as Bingley fell in love with her (p.192B; p.219R). Darcy admits that he communicated this interpretation of Jane's feelings to Bingley himself.

Q In his letter, Darcy appears more affronted by Elizabeth's accusations regarding his treatment of Wickham than those relating to Jane and Bingley. Why?

Chapter 36

Summary: *Elizabeth considers the contents of Darcy's letter.*

Elizabeth dismisses Darcy's interpretation of events between Bingley and Jane, crediting his actions yet again to his pride. She is more disconcerted by his account of his dealings with Wickham. That the particulars of Darcy's version of events accord generally with those of Wickham's is enough to allow her to entertain some doubt. She is unable to summon evidence to refute Darcy's version, realising she actually knows very little of Wickham's history.

Q What other evidence does Elizabeth gather to support Darcy's claims?

Chapter 37

Summary: *Darcy and Colonel Fitzwilliam leave Rosings; Elizabeth continues to reflect on Darcy's letter.*

Darcy's departure and her own impending return home prompt Elizabeth to further reflection, considering, in particular, the truth of Darcy's criticisms of her mother and sisters. Elizabeth offers no apology for her family here and finds little prospect of any improvement in their behaviour. This acknowledgement, combined with her sense of loss over Jane's relationship with Bingley, and Elizabeth's awareness of her own foolishness regarding Wickham, casts a despondent mood over this chapter.

Chapter 38

Summary: *Elizabeth and Maria leave Hunsford.*

Although eager to return home, Elizabeth feels some regret at abandoning Charlotte to the company of her husband. Mr Collins' long parting speeches show there has been no change in his character. Elizabeth accepts, however, that her friend is happy in her choice.

Chapter 39

Summary: *Kitty and Lydia meet Elizabeth, Jane and Maria on their journey home.*

This chapter returns us to Bennet family life. The rowdy dinner with the Lucases at Longbourn – with Mrs Bennet and Lydia shouting down the table – confirms Elizabeth's recent apprehensions about her family. Lydia, in particular, is presented in more detail in this chapter; she is shown to be uninhibited, pleasure-seeking and difficult to control.

Chapter 40

Summary: *Elizabeth tells Jane of Darcy's letter.*

Elizabeth is relieved to unburden herself to Jane by sharing the revelations in Darcy's letter. Jane is made a focus in this chapter as Elizabeth works to convince her that it is impossible for both Darcy and Wickham to come out favourably, revealing the flaw in Jane's desire to see the good in all. This chapter also makes clear that Jane's attachment to Bingley is genuine and she has been significantly troubled by the outcome of the relationship.

Chapter 41

Summary: *Lydia is invited to Brighton with Mrs Forster; Elizabeth takes leave of Wickham.*

Returned to the close proximity of her family, Elizabeth is able to observe their behaviours and attitudes. She now sees them through Darcy's eyes – where previously their follies had humoured her they now provoke shame. Her anxiety surrounding her family is made more acute when Lydia is invited to accompany Mrs Forster and the regiment on a visit to Brighton. Free from family influence, Lydia will be able to indulge in silliness and flirtation unchecked and Elizabeth urges their father to forbid the visit.

Q Why does Mr Bennet allow Lydia to go to Brighton?

Chapter 42

Summary: *Elizabeth and the Gardiners depart for Derbyshire.*

Rather than allowing herself to dwell on her family dynamics, Elizabeth looks forward to her holiday in the Lake District with the Gardiners. Mr Gardiner's business affairs force them to cut short their holiday, allowing them only to take in Derbyshire, Darcy's home county. Their point of focus within the county will be Lambton, only five miles from Pemberley, Darcy's estate. At the close of Volume Two, Pemberley is presented for both Elizabeth and the reader as a site of curiosity. In a way, the house stands in for Darcy himself here, enhancing interest in his character.

Q Examine the meditation on the Bennet marriage that opens this chapter. What are the effects of including this commentary at this point in the novel?

Volume Three Chapter 43

Summary: *Mrs Reynolds shows Elizabeth and the Gardiners over Pemberley; Darcy unexpectedly appears.*

This chapter opens with the observation that Elizabeth's spirits are 'in a high flutter' (p.235B; p.269R) at the prospect of visiting Pemberley – thus the first sentence of Volume Three suggests a shift in her attitude to Darcy. Elizabeth is intensely distressed by the sudden appearance of Darcy and concerned at how he might interpret her visit to his house. She is also disconcerted by his change in attitude, including his civility and his inquiries after her family. She anticipates his pride will be affronted by the presence of Mr and Mrs Gardiner, yet is immediately confused by his warmth towards them. Everything in Darcy's manner suggests his desire to maintain acquaintance with Elizabeth – not least his request to introduce his sister to her.

KEY POINT

Elizabeth approves of the 'natural' beauty of Pemberley's grounds, feeling an immediate affinity with this place. She also notes the housekeeper is 'less fine' and 'more civil' (p.236B; p.270R) than she had anticipated. The lack of affectation in the grounds, the staff and even the interior decoration of the estate challenge her earlier impressions of Darcy.

Chapter 44

Summary: *Elizabeth is introduced to Georgiana Darcy.*

The narrative perspective is filtered through Mr and Mrs Gardiner early in this chapter; they thus become the reader's witnesses. They identify a possible attachment between Darcy and Elizabeth and eventually have their suspicions confirmed. Meanwhile, Elizabeth discerns Bingley's continued interest in Jane and notes the changes in Darcy's demeanour, particularly his attitude to the 'very relations whom he had openly disdained' (p.251B; p.288R).

KEY POINT

At the close of this chapter Elizabeth considers her feelings for Darcy. She no longer feels 'hatred' (p.252B; p.290R) or 'dislike' (p.253B; p.291R) and is more willing to acknowledge his good qualities. Furthermore she expresses 'gratitude' towards him for the consideration he stills holds for her (p.253B; p.291R).

Chapter 45

Summary: *Mrs Gardiner and Elizabeth call on Georgiana at Pemberley.*

Darcy's feelings towards Elizabeth are further demonstrated during her visit to his sister. There is also a change in Caroline Bingley's attitude towards Elizabeth. Caroline has begun to appreciate Elizabeth as a real threat. As a result, Caroline's comments seem designed not only to remind the group – and Elizabeth herself – of Elizabeth's low social standing, but also to ensure that Elizabeth's entanglement with Wickham is apparent to all.

Chapter 46

Summary: *Jane writes several letters to Elizabeth regarding Lydia's disappearance with Wickham.*

This chapter ushers in the great crisis of the novel, namely Lydia's disappearance with Wickham. In the first letter it is presumed the couple plan to marry; this interpretation presents Lydia's action as unfortunate but not completely reprehensible. Jane suggests that it even casts Wickham in a favourable light, as he must know Lydia has no fortune and therefore the relationship is presumably based on real emotion. Jane's second letter has an entirely different tone, as it follows the revelation that Wickham does not intend to marry Lydia. This is truly disturbing news; if a woman of Lydia's station were to spend such time alone with a man, it would utterly ruin her reputation. The distress this news causes Elizabeth demonstrates the seriousness of the situation. As she tells Darcy, her anguish is compounded by a sense of responsibility for not conveying her own knowledge of Wickham's character to her family.

Chapter 47

Summary: *Elizabeth discusses Lydia's situation with Mr and Mrs Gardiner; Elizabeth returns to Longbourn.*

Elizabeth's attempts to find some hope in Lydia's situation only result in her feeling more distraught. She becomes thoroughly certain that Wickham is unlikely to choose Lydia as a wife, and feels sure that Lydia is willing to embark on a dangerous romance with him. Elizabeth returns to Longbourn to find her family in a state of chaos. Their only source of hope is that they will receive news of Wickham and Lydia having been married.

Chapter 48

Summary: *Mr Gardiner joins Mr Bennet in London to help search for Lydia; Elizabeth and Jane await news from Mr Gardiner; Mr Bennet returns to Longbourn.*

We witness wider responses to Lydia and Wickham's situation. The latter is now considered a villain in the eyes of the inhabitants of Meryton, despite the fact that 'but three months before' they had considered Wickham 'almost an angel of light' (p.279B; p.323R). Mr Collins writes to the family of his and Lady Catherine's opinions on the matter. The views expressed in his letter are extreme but not uncommon for the period, and it is perhaps the awareness of such judgements in the community that underlies the Bennet family's distress.

KEY POINT

Elizabeth considers how Lydia's actions have impacted on her feelings about the situation with Darcy. She feels greater distress because she believes Lydia's actions have cost her Darcy's good regard. Interestingly, Elizabeth accepts his perceived position as natural and does not criticise him for it.

Chapter 49

Summary: *Mr Gardiner sends news of Lydia and Wickham's impending marriage.*

Mr Gardiner writes to the Bennets that he has negotiated a settlement that will see Wickham marry Lydia. This returns Lydia's situation from one of ruined reputation to one where the familiar business terms of marriage are central. Mr Gardiner also informs them that Wickham's financial position is not as dire as previously assumed, and the couple will have something to live on once the debts have been settled. Mr Bennet is troubled by the arrangements. He presumes his brother-in-law has provided further compensation, and is anxious about how the debt will be repaid.

Chapter 50

Summary: *Mr Gardiner sends news that Wickham is to be stationed in the north of the county; Mr Bennet concedes that the newlyweds may visit Longbourn after the wedding.*

Now that the Lydia–Wickham crisis has been resolved, Elizabeth reflects on the issue of Darcy. She supposes that even if she had been able to conceal her sister's rash behaviour, the fact of Lydia's marriage to Wickham would preclude a relationship with Darcy.

Chapter 51

Summary: Lydia and Wickham are married and visit the Bennets at Longbourn.

Lydia seems wholly unchanged by her experience. She expresses no sense of shame and instead glories in her new position and its privileges. Elizabeth is disgusted with her sister and desires to say as little as possible to her about the marriage. Lydia persists and Elizabeth is rewarded with the astonishing knowledge that Darcy was present at the wedding.

Chapter 52

Summary: Elizabeth receives news from Mrs Gardiner of Darcy's involvement in Lydia and Wickham's affair.

Elizabeth discovers that it was Darcy who found Wickham and Lydia and insisted on providing the financial support needed to bribe Wickham into the marriage. Darcy bases his desire to help on his guilt in not having disclosed his knowledge of Wickham's character. This echoes Elizabeth's self-blame in Chapter 46. Mrs Gardiner's letter clearly conveys her belief that Darcy has another motive, which she makes explicit at the end of the letter by referring to Elizabeth as the future mistress of Pemberley.

Chapter 53

Summary: Lydia and Wickham depart; Darcy and Bingley visit Longbourn.

This chapter returns the suitors to the action. Elizabeth is shown moving through a complex series of emotions here. She is confused as to the motives of the two men in visiting Longbourn, grateful to Darcy for his actions concerning Lydia, and ashamed at her mother's rudeness towards him. She also expresses regret over the development of events, and concern over Darcy's silence, ultimately acknowledging to herself her feelings for him.

Chapter 54

Summary: Darcy and Bingley attend dinner at Longbourn.

In this chapter we witness Elizabeth and Darcy negotiating each other in the drawing room as their attempts to meet are thwarted or unsatisfactory. The reader's frustration at these mis-meetings are fuelled by Elizabeth's own sense of frustration; her desire to be with Darcy matches the reader's desire for their union. Elizabeth and Darcy's metaphorical dance around each other is contrasted with Jane and Bingley's steadier, more unified movement, as they sit serenely side by side.

Chapter 55

Summary: *Bingley and Jane are engaged.*

Here we see Mrs Bennet's comic attempts to leave Jane and Bingley alone together to allow him to propose. Once secured, the proposal produces the expected happiness and approval. It allows the confusion regarding the obstacles to the relationship to be cleared up. We learn, for example, that Bingley's sisters had not informed him of Jane's presence in London and that he had therefore assumed she was not interested in him.

Chapter 56

Summary: *Lady Catherine visits Longbourn to confront Elizabeth.*

The prospect of an engagement between Darcy and Elizabeth seems increasingly likely with the sudden appearance of Lady Catherine at Longbourn. She has come expressly to hear the truth of rumours of such an engagement. That Lady Catherine would travel to Longbourn for this purpose shows the strength of her concerns. Her objections to a possible engagement are twofold: namely that Darcy is intended for her own daughter and that Elizabeth is not a suitable match for her nephew. Elizabeth shows extraordinary spirit in rejecting all of Lady Catherine's arguments.

Chapter 57

Summary: *Mr Collins writes to Mr Bennet, hinting at Darcy's engagement to Elizabeth.*

Elizabeth ponders Lady Catherine's visit; she now views the older woman as a real threat to a possible relationship with Darcy, as Lady Catherine is presumably able to play on his insecurities, building on the objections to the relationship with Elizabeth that he himself had recognised. Elizabeth therefore resolves to interpret Darcy's continued absence as a sign of Lady Catherine's influence.

Chapter 58

Summary: *Darcy renews his offer to Elizabeth – and is accepted.*

This chapter finally brings Elizabeth and Darcy alone together. Elizabeth steers the conversation in a more intimate direction by thanking Darcy for his involvement in the Lydia–Wickham affair. His admission that he was motivated principally out of concern for Elizabeth – rather than guilt regarding Wickham – smoothes the way for his (second) declaration of love: a declaration that is, at last, reciprocated.

Q The second proposal is conveyed in third-person narrative rather than direct dialogue. What are the effects of this choice?

Chapter 59

Summary: *Elizabeth's engagement to Darcy is announced.*

This chapter is constructed as a series of episodes depicting the reaction to Elizabeth and Darcy's engagement. We witness Jane's incredulity and her concern over the true motives for Elizabeth's acceptance of the proposal. In the next episode, Mrs Bennet's vehement denunciations of Darcy set her up for the coming revelation, which is made to both parents in the third episode. Mr Bennet's initial reaction is similar to Jane's; he expresses concern over this seemingly sudden shift in Elizabeth's attitude to Darcy. Mrs Bennet, meanwhile, is rendered speechless for the first time in the novel (p.357B; p.416R).

Chapter 60

Summary: *Elizabeth and Darcy discuss their relationship; news of the engagement spreads.*

The light conversational mode adopted by Elizabeth and Darcy masks some serious issues in this chapter. Elizabeth teases Darcy about the development of his feelings for her, positing her indifference as the basis for his interest. Her tone is carefree but touches on an interesting point – that she attracted his attention by acting against accepted notions of proper feminine behaviour.

Chapter 61

Summary: *Follow-up of the principal characters.*

The final chapter provides a snapshot of developments in the lives of the principal characters following Jane's and Elizabeth's marriages. These snapshots offer few surprises, merely confirming our earlier interpretations. Thus Lydia and Wickham remain flighty and dissolute; Miss Bingley supercilious; and Lady Catherine outraged.

CHARACTERS & RELATIONSHIPS

Mr Bennet

Key Quotes

'Mr Bennet was so odd a mixture of quick parts, sarcastic humour, reserve, and caprice, that the experience of three and twenty years had been insufficient to make his wife understand his character.' (p.7B; p.5R)

'He was fond of the country and of books; and from these tastes had arisen his principal enjoyments. To his wife he was very little otherwise indebted, than as her ignorance and folly had contributed to his amusement.' (p.228B; p.261R)

Mr Bennet does not appear to play an active role in the social events of the Meryton community. He spends much of his time in his library, away from the irritating conversation of his wife and younger daughters. He treats his wife as an object of amusement and seems to have little in common with her. His reactions to Mr Collins reveal his sense of humour, which Elizabeth alone seems to appreciate. The sympathy that exists between these two characters is clearly drawn and she is identified as his favourite; this makes her criticisms of his qualities as a husband and father all the more striking. In Chapter 41 she speaks of the possibility that Lydia will 'soon be beyond the reach of amendment' and identifies Mr Bennet as the only means of averting catastrophe (p.223B; p.255R).

Interestingly, neither Mr nor Mrs Bennet are individualised with first names. This strengthens their identity as 'husband/father' and 'wife/mother' and also, perhaps, encourages our critique of their fulfilment of these roles.

Mrs Bennet

key quotes

'She was a woman of mean understanding, little information, and uncertain temper.' (p.7B; p.5R)

'Well, my comfort is, I am sure Jane will die of a broken heart, and then he will be sorry for what he has done.' (Mrs Bennet, p.220B; p.251R)

Mrs Bennet is an emotional, nervy woman who demonstrates little sense. She is driven by the 'business' of finding husbands for her daughters; her pursuit of this object leads her at times to ridiculous actions, such as forcing Jane to walk to Netherfield. When it started to rain heavily on Jane's journey to Netherfield, her 'sisters were uneasy for her, but her mother was delighted' (pp.31–2B; p.34R). Her response suggests a callous attitude to her daughter's immediate welfare.

The narrative offers direct criticism of Mrs Bennet. In Chapter 47 the narrator lays responsibility for Lydia's behaviour on her mother. Upon news of the girl's departure with Wickham, Mrs Bennet blames 'every body but the person to whose ill judging indulgence the errors of her daughter must be principally owing' (p.273B; p.314R).

There is another side to Mrs Bennet's character, as Austen's biographer Clare Tomalin reminds us: 'Lizzy's vitality – and Lydia's too – comes from their mother, who is not, as she is often represented, a frumpish elderly woman but one in her forties who would like to be taken to Brighton to enjoy herself' (Tomalin 1997, p.162). Perhaps Elizabeth's discomfort with her sister and mother derives in part from her recognition of the traits she shares with them.

Jane Bennet

key quotes

'You never see a fault in any body. All the world are good and agreeable in your eyes. I never heard you speak ill of a human being in my life.' (Elizabeth, p.16B; p.15R)

'Neither could [Elizabeth] deny the justice of [Darcy's] description of Jane. – She felt that Jane's feelings, though fervent, were little displayed, and that there was a constant complacency in her air and manner, not often united with great sensibility.' (p.202B; p.230R)

The eldest Bennet daughter is a quiet, reserved individual with a gentle, loving nature. Despite their differences in temperament she shares a special bond with Elizabeth. Whilst Elizabeth actively critiques those around her, Jane is determined to see the good in everyone. This trait makes her minor criticism of Caroline Bingley in Chapter 26 ('I cannot help blaming her. She was very wrong in singling me out as she did', p.146B; p.167R) compelling evidence of strong emotion.

Elizabeth Bennet

KEY QUOTES

'There are few people whom I really love, and still fewer of whom I think well. The more I see of the world, the more dissatisfied I am with it; and every day confirms my belief of the inconsistency of all human characters, and of the little dependence that can be placed on the appearance of either merit or sense.' (Elizabeth, p.133B; p.153R)

'But vanity, not love, has been my folly – Pleased with the preference of one, and offended by the neglect of the other, on the very beginning of our acquaintance, I have courted prepossession and ignorance, and driven reason away, where either were concerned. Till this moment, I never knew myself.' (Elizabeth, p.202B; p.229R)

Elizabeth is a vibrant, intelligent and strong-willed young woman. She has a teasing, playful personality that reflects aspects of both parents. Like her father, she refuses to take things seriously ('I dearly love a laugh', p.56B; p.62R). She shares her mother's desire for amusement and diversion, and it is perhaps his ability to provide these that attracts her to Wickham.

The novel offers repeated indications of Elizabeth's unconventional character, including her teasing conversations with Darcy, her determination to attend to her sister during her illness, her refusal of Mr Collins and – initially – of Darcy, and her attitude to Lady Catherine.

Elizabeth considers herself an observer of human nature. We receive her measured assessments of characters such as Charlotte Lucas and Charles Bingley – it is in reference to these individuals that she makes her comment regarding the 'inconsistency' of those around her (p.133B; p.153R). However it is the 'inconsistencies' in her own character that she must ultimately come to terms with. She finds her hasty judgements of

Darcy and Wickham inaccurate and realises she was led to believe the latter and discredit the former out of 'vanity' (p.202B; p.229R).

The major adjustment Elizabeth has to make concerns her relations with Darcy. Part of this adjustment requires her to look critically at her family dynamics. When she returns to Longbourn from Hunsford she witnesses Mrs Bennet, Kitty and Lydia lamenting over the departure of the regiment. Where their silliness might previously have amused her, it now provokes 'shame' and prompts her to feel 'anew the justice of Mr Darcy's objections' (p.221B; p.254R). Following her engagement she finds it necessary to actively censor Darcy's conduct with certain members of her family and to look 'forward with delight to the time when they should be removed from society so little pleasing to either' (p.363B; p.423R).

Mary Bennet

Key Quotes

'Mary wished to say something very sensible, but knew not how.' (p.9B; p.7R)

'Mary, who having, in consequence of being the only plain one in the family, worked hard for knowledge and accomplishments, was always impatient for display.' (p.25B; p.27R)

Mary has established herself as the 'intellectual' of the family and spends her time reading 'great books' and making 'extracts' (p.9B; p.7R). She also considers herself an accomplished musician, although Elizabeth's responses to her sister's playing suggest the gap between the younger woman's understanding of her talent and her actual ability. Mary is a rather humourless and moralistic individual; she shares these qualities with Mr Collins and is the only one of the sisters to entertain the possibility of a relationship with him (p.122B; p.139R).

Catherine (Kitty) Bennet

Key Quotes

'Don't keep coughing so, Kitty, for heaven's sake! Have a little compassion on my nerves. You tear them to pieces.' (Mrs Bennet, p.8B; p.6R)

'Kitty then owned, with a very natural triumph on knowing more than the rest of us, that in Lydia's last letter, she had prepared her for such a step. She had known, it seems, of their being in love with each other, many weeks.' (Jane, p.276B; p.318R)

The fourth Bennet daughter, Kitty, is the least defined in the novel. We learn that she is 'slight and delicate' (p.277B; p.320R), and her repeated coughing drives Mrs Bennet to distraction. Her weaker constitution may be why she has assumed the position of follower to the younger but more robust Lydia. In Chapter 7 a slight distinction is drawn between these two sisters. Their rapturous reaction to the news of the military regiment being stationed at Meryton draws a scathing response from Mr Bennet. Whilst Lydia greets her father's admonishment with 'indifference', Kitty is 'disconcerted' by it (p.30B; p.32R). Chapter 61 informs us that once Kitty is separated from Lydia and exposed more exclusively to the influence of Jane and Elizabeth, the differences between the two are strengthened, and Kitty's behaviour improves.

Lydia Bennet

Key Quotes

'Lydia was a stout, well-grown girl of fifteen, with a fine complexion and good-humoured countenance; a favourite with her mother, whose affection had brought her into public at an early age.' (p.45B; pp.49–50R)

'Lord! how I should like to be married before any of you; and then I would chaperon you about to all the balls.' (Lydia, p.213B; p.243R)

'… she has never been taught to think on serious subjects; and for the last half year, nay, for a twelvemonth, she has been given up to nothing but amusement and vanity. She has been allowed to dispose of her time in the most idle and frivolous manner, and to adopt any opinions that came in her way.' (Elizabeth, p.269B; pp.310–11R)

The youngest sister is a headstrong, pleasure-seeking girl preoccupied with parties, friends and fashion. She seems impervious to control or criticism and is utterly unfazed by the distress and embarrassment her departure with Wickham brings to her family. Upon her return to Longbourn in Chapter 51, the narrator notes: 'Lydia was Lydia still; untamed, unabashed, wild, noisy, and fearless' (p.298B; p.345R).

Fitzwilliam Darcy

Key Quotes

'Mr Darcy soon drew the attention of the room by his fine, tall person, handsome features, noble mein; and the report which was in general circulation within five minutes after his entrance, of his having ten thousand a year.' (p.12B; p.10R)

'I certainly have not the talent which some people possess ... of conversing easily with those I have never seen before. I cannot catch their tone of conversation, or appear interested in their concerns, as I often see done.' (Darcy, p.171B; p.196R)

Handsome, reserved Darcy captures the attention of Elizabeth, the villagers of Meryton and the reader of *Pride and Prejudice*. His fortune and status lend him glamour, whilst his inscrutable manner brings an air of mystery. We see both Caroline Bingley and Elizabeth trying to work him out.

Darcy's unsociable nature soon draws the scorn of the Meryton community. Along with his lack of sociability, Darcy is divided from Elizabeth by his pride. This aspect of his character is revealed in his first proposal to her. He expresses his awareness of her family's 'inferiority' and of the 'degradation' of a connection with them (p.185B; p.210R). His continued contact with Elizabeth and his growing acquaintance with the Gardiners encourages him to reassess his position. By the time of the second proposal he considers his earlier behaviour 'unpardonable' and 'cannot think of it without abhorrence' (p.347B; p.404R).

Q How do you account for Darcy's change in attitude between his first and second proposals?

Charles Bingley

Key Quotes

'Mr Bingley was good looking and gentlemanlike; he had a pleasant countenance, and easy, unaffected manners.' (p.12B; p.10R)

'Bingley has great natural modesty, with a stronger dependence on my judgement than on his own.' (Darcy, p.193B; p.220R)

Charles Bingley is a warm and friendly young man. He welcomes new acquaintances and seems unconcerned by issues of rank. Darcy's friendship with Bingley is grounded on a respect for the 'easiness, openness, ductility of his temper' (p.18B; p.17R). Meanwhile, Bingley values Darcy's opinions and judgements to the extent that he acts on the other's advice even when it impacts negatively on him. Bingley's temperament is well-matched with that of his eventual wife, Jane Bennet.

Caroline Bingley and Louisa Hurst

Key Quote

'They were in fact very fine ladies; not deficient in good humour when they were pleased, nor in the power of being agreeable where they chose it; but proud and conceited.' (p.17B; p.16R)

Caroline is a cold and supercilious woman, acutely conscious of the status her wealth affords. Drawn to Jane's gentle, dignified manner, Caroline befriends her but develops a strained relationship with Elizabeth. Miss Bingley's animosity towards the latter grows more pronounced as she becomes aware of her position as rival for Darcy's affections.

Louisa is less defined than Caroline, but shares her sister's superior attitude. She is married to Mr Hurst, of whom we learn little more than that he is 'an indolent man, who lived only to eat, drink, and play at cards' (p.35B; p.38R).

Charlotte Lucas

Key Quotes

'Happiness in marriage is entirely a matter of chance.' (Charlotte, p.24B; p.25R)

'I ask only a comfortable home; and considering Mr Collins's character, connections, and situation in life, I am convinced that my chance of happiness with him is as fair, as most people can boast on entering the marriage state.' (Charlotte, p.123B; p.140R)

Charlotte is Elizabeth's close friend and confidante but there are significant differences between them. Charlotte is a realist, with a more prosaic attitude to romance than Elizabeth's. Although aware of her friend's antipathy to (dislike for) Darcy, Charlotte cautions her 'not to be a simpleton and allow her fancy for Wickham to make her appear unpleasant in the eyes of a man of ten times his consequence' (p.89B; p.102R).

At 27, Charlotte is in a more precarious position than the Bennet sisters and marriage for love is less important to her than securing a comfortable future. Her awareness of her situation prompts her to accept Mr Collins' proposal, a development that shocks Elizabeth and strains their friendship.

Mr Collins

Key Quotes

'He was a tall, heavy looking young man of five and twenty. His air was grave and stately, and his manners were very formal.' (p.63B; p.72R)

'... his veneration for [Lady Catherine] as his patroness, mingling with a very good opinion of himself, of his authority as a clergyman, and his rights as a rector, made him altogether a mixture of pride and obsequiousness, self-importance and humility.' (p.69B; p.78R)

Mr Collins is a self-important, moralistic individual seemingly devoid of any sense of humour. His reverent attitude to his patroness, Lady Catherine, renders him a ridiculous figure. Mr Bennet is particularly amused by his young cousin and teases out of him the damning fact that he prepares his compliments to Lady Catherine in advance. His attentions to the Bennet daughters stem from Lady Catherine's influence, as she has urged him to marry.

Mr Wickham

Key Quotes

'His appearance was greatly in his favour; he had all the best part of beauty, a fine countenance, a good figure, and very pleasing address.' (p.71B; p.80R)

'All Meryton seemed striving to blacken the man, who, but three months before, had been almost an angel of light.' (p.279B; pp.322–3R)

Mr Wickham is handsome, intelligent and gregarious. His sociable nature makes him a welcome addition to the neighbourhood – in striking contrast to Darcy. Witnessing Elizabeth as she succumbs to his charms helps the reader understand how he has been able to manipulate others, such as the late Mr Darcy and Georgiana, and how he will seduce Lydia.

Darcy's letter to Elizabeth in Chapter 35 represents the first really negative appraisal of Wickham in the novel. The letter portrays Wickham as an unscrupulous, conniving charmer who gained the confidence of his father and sister but never Darcy himself. As Darcy's letter influences Elizabeth's perspective on her family, so it does her attitude to Wickham – where previously she had seen 'gentleness' she now recognises 'affectation' (p.225B; p.257R).

Sir William Lucas and Maria Lucas

Sir William's self-important air and reverence for nobility renders him a figure of fun in the Meryton community. He remains nevertheless an amiable individual, by 'nature inoffensive, friendly and obliging' (p.19B; p.19R).

His younger daughter, Maria, accompanies Sir William and Elizabeth on their visit to Charlotte at Hunsford parsonage. We learn little of Maria's character beyond the fact that she, like her father, is awed by the grandeur of Rosings Park.

Lady Catherine de Bourgh

Key Quotes

'Her air was not conciliating, nor was her manner of receiving them, such as to make her visitors forget their inferior rank.' (p.159B; p.183R)

'I have not been used to submit to any person's whims. I have not been in the habit of brooking disappointment.' (p.336B; p.391R)

Lady Catherine is a haughty, garrulous and opinionated woman. She spends her days distributing orders and unwelcome advice. Her comfortable existence is unsettled by Elizabeth's presence. The latter poses an obstacle to the older woman's plans to have Darcy marry her daughter Anne: a timid, delicate and sickly individual. Lady Catherine is also an archetypal snob and objects to a woman of Elizabeth's class and connections marrying into the family.

Mr and Mrs Gardiner

Key Quote

'Mr Gardiner was a sensible, gentlemanlike man, greatly superior to his sister as well by nature as education.' (p.137B; p.158R)

Key Quote

'Mrs Gardiner ... was an amiable, intelligent, elegant woman, and a great favourite with all her Longbourn nieces. Between the two eldest and herself especially, there subsisted a very particular regard.' (p.137B; p.158R)

Mr Gardiner is a merchant of some description and the family derive their living from trade: a fact that garners the disdain of the Bingley sisters. However, their intelligence, amiability and common sense draw Darcy to them. Mrs Gardiner acts as confidante to Elizabeth once relations with Charlotte have become strained. The easy friendship Elizabeth shares with Mrs Gardiner contrasts sharply with the Elizabeth's attitude to her own mother.

Colonel Fitzwilliam

Darcy's cousin Colonel Fitzwilliam is a pleasant, sociable man who forms a friendship with Elizabeth during their stay at Rosings Park. He challenges her earlier impressions of Darcy but also provides the crucial news of his cousin's interference in a friend's relationship. Elizabeth correctly recognises the relationship as the one between Jane and Bingley.

Georgiana Darcy

Georgiana is a gentle, reserved young woman. The narrator notes that her manner may seem aloof to strangers, but Elizabeth and Mrs Gardiner recognise that instead it comes from shyness and 'the fear of doing wrong' (p.255B; p.293R). Georgiana quickly warms to Elizabeth and at the novel's close it is noted that they have formed a strong bond.

Colonel and Mrs Forster

Colonel Forster leads the militia regiment. His young wife and Lydia share a 'resemblance in good humour and good spirits' (p.222B; p.254R). In response to Elizabeth's misgivings about the Brighton trip, Mr Bennet claims Colonel Forster is 'a sensible man' and expects he will keep Lydia 'out of real mischief' (p.224B; p.256R). Colonel Forster later provides evidence of Wickham's true character and regrets that he did not interfere more forcefully in the latter's dealings with Lydia.

Mrs Reynolds

Mrs Reynolds' principal function in the novel is to provide an alternative assessment of Darcy. Although Mr and Mrs Gardiner joke about Mrs Reynolds' glowing commendations of her master, Elizabeth recognises her authority to judge Darcy and is impressed and swayed by her claims.

THEMES, IDEAS & VALUES

Marriage

Key Quotes

'It is a truth universally acknowledged, that a single man in possession of a good fortune, must be in want of a wife.' (p.5B; p.3R)

'I ask only a comfortable home; and considering Mr Collins's character, connections, and situation in life, I am convinced that my chance of happiness with him is as fair, as most people can boast on entering the marriage state.' (Charlotte, p.123B; p.140R)

'[Elizabeth] began now to comprehend that he was exactly the man, who, in disposition and talents, would most suit her … It was an union that must have been to the advantage of both; by her ease and liveliness, his mind might have been softened, his manners improved, and from his judgement, information, and knowledge of the world, she must have received benefit of greater importance.' (p.295B; p.342R)

'But how little of permanent happiness could belong to a couple who were only brought together because their passions were stronger than their virtue …' (p.296B; p.342R)

Marriage drives the plot of Pride and Prejudice. The story is constructed around a group of sisters whose future security and comfort depends on their ability to make 'good' marriages. Not only is their family estate entailed away from them (passing through the male line) but their father has neglected to save sufficient funds to allow them to live comfortably independently. Although Pride and Prejudice is written with a lightness of touch and includes much humour, we should not disregard the seriousness of the Bennet girls' predicament.

In light of these circumstances, Elizabeth's rejection of Mr Collins' offer of marriage – although perfectly natural to a modern sensibility – appears somewhat reckless. Her attitude is contrasted with that of Charlotte Lucas, who readily accepts Mr Collins' proposal with full knowledge of his true character. Elizabeth is shocked at Charlotte's actions, believing her friend has 'sacrificed every better feeling to worldly advantage' (p.123B; p.141R). Charlotte, however, is in a more precarious position than Elizabeth. She is seven years older and with seemingly even less chance of family support. This is indicated by the fact that her family can only finance one daughter on the marriage market (her sisters are not yet 'out' in society) compared to the Bennet family (all five sisters are 'out'). Significant stigma was attached to an unmarried woman of Charlotte's age; she was considered 'a burden and, in many eyes, an incomplete woman' (Olsen 2005, p.426).

Charlotte Lucas' situation offers a sustained examination of the importance of marriage in a woman's status and lifestyle. Charlotte admits she is not a 'romantic' (p.123B; p.140R) and has accepted Mr Collins 'solely from the pure and disinterested desire of an establishment' (p.120B; p.137R). The narrative tells us 'marriage had always been her object; it was the only honourable provision for well-educated young women of small fortune, and however uncertain of giving happiness, must be their pleasantest preservative from want' (p.120B; p.138R). The benefits of Charlotte's marriage for the wider Lucas family are also depicted. For a start, it will allow her younger sisters to step into the courting game earlier. Furthermore, had Charlotte remained unmarried at the death of her father, her younger brothers would have been responsible for supporting her – with her marriage, Mr Collins now assumes this role. Ultimately, the relatively autonomous position of a wife is more attractive than that of a dependent daughter or sister.

In spite of her attitude to Charlotte's decision, Elizabeth does recognise the economic imperatives that govern the choice of spouse in her society. In Chapter 26 she notes that Kitty and Lydia have taken the news of Wickham's attachment to the wealthy Miss King 'much more to heart than I do. They are young in the ways of the world, and not yet open to the mortifying conviction that handsome young men must have something to live on, as well as the plain' (p.148B; p.170R).

Yet whilst *Pride and Prejudice* presents marriage to a less-than-ideal partner as an economic necessity for some women (and some men), it also cautions against incompatibility in marriage. The most striking example of this is the narrative's judgement of the Bennet parents' marriage. This union is represented as one fundamentally wanting in mutual interests or even basic respect. Captivated by his prospective wife's 'youth', 'beauty' and 'appearance of good humour', Mr Bennet failed to notice her 'weak understanding and illiberal mind' (p.228B; p.261R) before he married her. His disdain for her intellectual abilities and emotionalism has led him to treat her as an object of amusement. Elizabeth is acutely aware of this and regrets his habit of ridiculing Mrs Bennet in front of their children. When Elizabeth announces her engagement to Darcy, her father cautions her against entering a marriage lacking respect. His comments are also a reflection on his own situation: 'Your lively talents would place you in the greatest danger in an unequal marriage … My child, let me not have the grief of seeing *you* unable to respect your partner in life' (p.356B; p.415R).

The novel also offers a sobering assessment of the consequences of Wickham and Lydia's hasty union. As a relationship primarily founded on physical desire, it can be read as a replication of the Bennet parents' marriage, and like that earlier example it quickly dissolves: the narrative observes that Wickham's 'affection' for Lydia 'soon sunk into indifference; her's lasted a little longer' (p.366B; p.426R). Following Wickham's discharge from the militia, the couple find themselves 'always moving from place to place in quest of a cheap situation, and always spending more than they ought' (p.366B; p.426R). Lydia is denied the happy, settled existence of her eldest sisters.

The marriages that are presented positively in *Pride and Prejudice* are those based on shared temperament. Jane and Bingley are both amiable, unaffected individuals with a propensity to look for the good in all. Elizabeth can 'honestly and heartily' express 'delight' at the news of their engagement due to the 'general similarity of feeling and taste between' them (p.328B; p.382R). The more complex personalities of Elizabeth and Darcy are also well matched. Their spirited discussions demonstrate their shared intelligence and Elizabeth gradually recognises their common moral values. On her visit to Pemberley, she also approves of Darcy's aesthetic taste and expresses an affinity with his home environment. Furthermore, Elizabeth and Darcy each undergo a period of growth and adjustment that tests their feelings for one another and forges a stronger bond between them. In its final chapters, the narrative expresses certainty of the prosperous and happy futures these two couples will enjoy.

First impressions

Key Quotes

'… no sooner had [Darcy] made it clear to himself and his friends that [Elizabeth] had hardly a good feature in her face, than he began to find it was rendered uncommonly intelligent by the beautiful expression of her dark eyes … Of this she was perfectly unaware; to her he was only the man who made himself agreeable no where, and who had not thought her handsome enough to dance with.' (p.24B; pp.25–6R)

'[Elizabeth] perfectly remembered every thing that had passed in conversation between Wickham and herself, in their first evening at Mr Philips's … She was now struck with the impropriety of such communications to a stranger, and wondered it had escaped her before.' (p.200B; p.228R)

'How earnestly did [Elizabeth] then wish that her former opinions had been more reasonable, her expressions more moderate!' (p.355B; p.414R)

The early title of *Pride and Prejudice* provides a clue to one of its key themes. The possible danger of forming an opinion of another individual based on their initial presentation furthers the novel's plot. Elizabeth finds her first impressions of both Darcy and Wickham to be inaccurate. Darcy's pride and arrogance are shown to stem from reserve and misunderstanding, whilst Wickham's warmth and easy charm mask his self-interest. Over the course of the novel, Elizabeth learns to perform more complex and nuanced readings of character rather than relying on 'first impressions'.

Darcy, meanwhile, compromises the possibility of developing a relationship with Elizabeth when he inadvertently allows her to overhear his first impressions of her. His initial attitude to Elizabeth is a damning indictment of his own character for he performs a superficial assessment based on her appearance and perceived popularity: 'She is tolerable; but not handsome enough to tempt *me*; and I am in no humour at present to give consequence to young ladies who are slighted by other men' (p.13B; p.12R). Darcy must work to overcome the effects that this pronouncement has on Elizabeth (and also, perhaps, on the reader). *His* initial impressions are challenged early in the novel. Following a further encounter with Elizabeth in Chapter 6 we learn that he now finds her attractive and charming – his first impressions have been modified. Hers, however, remain fixed. She continues to consider him arrogant and unfriendly and interprets his sudden interest in her as 'satirical' (p.25B; p.26R).

Whilst Elizabeth and Darcy eventually find their first impressions – especially of each other – inadequate, other characters have theirs vindicated. Jane and Bingley's favourable initial impressions of each other are significantly challenged by the opinions of others but are ultimately affirmed. Their decision to marry is based on aspects of character they discerned in each other at their first meeting. Yet this aspect of the novel also perhaps reflects Jane and Bingley's relatively straightforward natures in comparison to the more complex personalities of Elizabeth and Darcy.

The events of Chapter 36 show Elizabeth's recognition of her own weaknesses in judging character, as she moves from unwillingness to believe Darcy's claims to an understanding of having been deceived by Wickham. As she ponders the contents of Darcy's letter, every 'lingering struggle in [Wickham's] favour' grows 'fainter and fainter' (p.201B; p.228R). She realises her own 'vanity' has coloured her initial assessments of these men:

> Pleased with the preference of the one, and offended by the neglect of the other, on the very beginning of our acquaintance, I have courted prepossession and ignorance, and driven reason away, where either were concerned. (p.202B; p.229R)

The remainder of the novel shows Elizabeth building further evidence to support her new estimations of Wickham and Darcy.

Pride and prejudice

'Pride … is a very common failing I believe … there are very few of us who do not cherish a feeling of self-complacency on the score of some quality or other, real or imaginary.' (Mary, p.21B; p.21R)

'I was spoilt by my parents, who though good themselves … allowed, encouraged, almost taught me to be selfish and overbearing, to care for none beyond my own family circle …' (Darcy, p.349B; p.406R)

'[Elizabeth] grew absolutely ashamed of herself – Of neither Darcy nor Wickham could she think, without feeling that she had been blind, partial, prejudiced, absurd.' (p.201B; p.229R)

'She explained what [the letter's] effect on her had been, and how gradually all her former prejudices had been removed.' (p.348B; p.405R)

Following his behaviour at the Meryton assembly, pride becomes the defining aspect of Darcy's character and draws the scorn of his new acquaintances: 'His character was decided. He was the proudest, most disagreeable man in the world, and every body hoped that he would never come there again' (p.13B; p.11R). The community's understanding of Darcy's pride relates it to his class position. Interestingly, Charlotte Lucas excuses Darcy's pride on this basis: 'One cannot wonder that so very fine a young man, with family, fortune, every thing in his favour, should think highly of himself'. He has, she suggests, 'a *right* to be proud' (p.21B; p.21R).

The Bennet family and their neighbours judge Darcy as 'proud' because, unlike Bingley, he refuses to mix with the community and seems aloof and arrogant. In Chapter 31, he excuses his behaviour as resulting from an inability to converse 'easily with those I have never seen before. I cannot catch their tone of conversation, or appear interested in their concerns, as I often see done' (p.171B; p.196R). His pride can thus be read as originating from reserve or social awkwardness. However, in Chapter 58 he also acknowledges that his sense of pride *had* been based on his awareness of his wealth and position. He tells Elizabeth that his parents had fostered in him from childhood a disdainful attitude to those of an inferior status (p.349B; p.406R).

The nature of Darcy's pride is strongly drawn in Chapter 34. Even after Elizabeth has raised the topic of Wickham, Darcy continues to focus instead on the 'natural and just' response to their different class status, asking her, 'could you expect me to rejoice in the inferiority of your connections?' (p.188B; p.214R). Once he leaves, it is the remembrance of his 'pride, his abominable pride' (p.189B; p.215R) that allows Elizabeth to quickly overcome 'the pity which the consideration of his attachment had for a moment excited' (p.189B; p.215R). Darcy's pride is thus established as the defining feature of his character and the key obstacle in winning Elizabeth's affections or furthering a relationship with her.

Alongside the effects of pride we also see the workings of prejudice in the novel. For example, the Bingley sisters are prejudiced against Jane because of her family connections, and Mrs Bennet is prejudiced against Darcy because of his superior attitude. Elizabeth is aware of the effects of prejudice in her society. In Chapter 18 she asks Darcy whether he allows his opinions of others 'to be blinded by prejudice', to which he replies: 'I hope not' (p.92B; p.105R). In fact, both characters' opinions are influenced by prejudice. Darcy's extreme pride in his own connections makes him prejudiced towards those lacking similar 'consequence' (p.95B; p.109R). Elizabeth's belief in the superiority of her own judgements allows her prejudices against Darcy to remain unchecked for much of the novel.

Class

Key Quotes

'Elizabeth's courage did not fail her. She had heard nothing of Lady Catherine that spoke her awful from any extraordinary talents or miraculous virtue, and the mere stateliness of money and rank, she thought she could witness without trepidation.' (p.158B; p.182R)

'Could you expect me to rejoice in the inferiority of your connections? To congratulate myself on the hope of relations, whose condition in life is so decidedly beneath my own?' (Darcy, p.188B; p.214R)

'In marrying your nephew, I should not consider myself as quitting that sphere. He is a gentleman; I am a gentleman's daughter; so far we are equal.' (Elizabeth, p.337B; p.392R)

The characters in *Pride and Prejudice* represent a range of class positions. Fitzwilliam Darcy and Lady Catherine de Bourgh, for example, are extremely wealthy members of the landed gentry. They come from distinguished families with connections to the nobility. They are thus the highest status characters in the novel according to the social hierarchy of the time. The Bingley family fortune derives from trade, which places them on a different social plane from the inheritors of grand estates such as Rosings Park and Pemberley. Charles Bingley has leased Netherfield Park with a view to establishing his own estate and thereby enhancing his status. His sisters are 'very anxious for his having an estate of his own' (p.17B; p.17R) as they retain a sense of insecurity about the origins, and perhaps even the future, of their fortune.

Much further down the hierarchy are characters such as the Gardiners, who live in an unfashionable part of London and earn a living from commercial activity. The Gardiners attract the disdain of Lady Catherine and – even more particularly – the Bingley sisters. The novel, however, does not share this disdain. It suggests, rather, the unreliability of class as an indicator of character. Lady Catherine and the Bingley sisters are repeatedly represented, despite their wealth and status, as stupid, shallow and self-absorbed. In the esteem with which they are held by Elizabeth and, ultimately, by Darcy, and in their concern for family as demonstrated by their involvement in the Lydia–Wickham affair, the Gardiners are shown to be sensible, intelligent and compassionate.

Ultimately, the Gardiners emerge as more productive members of society than those like Lady Catherine, who represent the old social order. Austen's text can therefore be read as a critique of traditional class systems. However, the novel also remains significantly interested in class, and Jane and Elizabeth are rewarded with marriages that will propel them up the social hierarchy. Juliet McMaster has noted this double perspective in Austen's work: 'The quality of humanity is to be judged by moral and humane standards, Austen suggests, not by social status; but like her own temporary snobs, Darcy and Emma [from the novel *Emma*], she pays full attention to class status first' (McMaster 1997, p.125).

Elizabeth demonstrates a complex range of attitudes to class. For example, she does not share Sir William's and Maria's awed reactions to the trappings of wealth on display at Rosings Park. And in Chapter 56 she is forthright in response to Lady Catherine's insults regarding her family and social status: '[Darcy] is a gentleman; I am a gentleman's daughter; so far we are equal' (p.337B; p.392R). A further example of Elizabeth's critical attitude to the class system occurs in Chapter 18. When Caroline Bingley refutes Wickham's claims against Darcy, Elizabeth interprets Caroline's judgement against Wickham as an example of class prejudice: 'I have heard you accuse him of nothing worse than of being the son of Mr Darcy's steward' (p.93B; p.106R). It is also important to note that as her relationship with Darcy progresses, although Elizabeth feels increasing shame in relation to her family, this is based not on their lack of status but their lack of propriety. She does not feel anxiety about the Gardiners' class position, but instead about her mother's and youngest sisters' uncontrolled emotion and wayward behaviour. The final chapter notes that the Gardiners are frequent and welcome visitors at Pemberley following Elizabeth and Darcy's marriage: Mrs Bennet and Lydia are not.

However, at other points in the novel, Elizabeth seems more influenced by class distinctions. In Chapter 18 she becomes anxious at Mr Collins' desire to introduce himself to Darcy, telling him the latter would 'consider his addressing him without introduction as an impertinent freedom' and that Darcy, as 'the superior in consequence' has the privilege of initiating the acquaintance (p.95B; p.109R).

Public conduct and reputation

Key Quotes

'... under such a misfortune as this, one cannot see too little of one's neighbours. Assistance is impossible; condolence, insufferable. Let them triumph over us at a distance, and be satisfied.' (Elizabeth, p.278B; pp.320–1R)

'If you were aware ... of the very great disadvantage to us all, which must arise from the public notice of Lydia's unguarded and imprudent manner; nay, which has already arisen from it, I am sure you would judge differently in the affair.' (Elizabeth, p.223B; p.255R)

Jane Austen illuminates the pettiness and spite circulating in the claustrophobic environment of the village. In Chapter 50 the news of Lydia and Wickham's marriage spreads 'quickly ... through the house;

and with proportionate speed through the neighbourhood'. The narrative suggests that, whilst the villagers were hoping for a more unfortunate outcome:

> the good-natured wishes for [Lydia's] well-doing, which had proceeded before … lost but little of their spirit in this change of circumstances, because with such an husband, her misery was considered certain. (p.293B; p.340R)

The description of 'the spiteful old ladies in Meryton' is comic, but also exposes the atmosphere of surveillance that operates in the village, and the delight the inhabitants quietly take in their neighbours' misfortunes (p.293B; p.340R).

Much of the action in *Pride and Prejudice* is structured around social events, from large, formal occasions such as the ball at Netherfield, to chance events such as Elizabeth's sojourn at Netherfield following Jane's illness or her unexpected meetings with Darcy in the grounds around Hunsford parsonage. These events bring the characters together in social settings of varying degrees of formality, allowing the novel to focus on character interaction – how the characters respond to each other in various environments. Thus the structure of *Pride and Prejudice* mimics that of the character's lives, which are also structured around these kinds of meetings. Attitudes to social obligation and ideas about appropriate public behaviour are of great importance in the world of the novel. Mr Bennet's obligation to introduce his family to Bingley, and the criticisms of Darcy's behaviour at social events, are two examples of this.

This focus on social settings means we witness the characters' social performances: how they choose to present themselves in public. The characters are under surveillance, not just by the reader but by those around them in the world of the novel. Much of our knowledge of key characters, including Mrs Bennet, Lydia, Mary and Darcy, is imparted through responses to their social performances. For example, Darcy is considered disagreeable because he will not comply with the social routines of the community with good grace: he has little interest in dancing, visiting, and playing cards. As these activities are the outward expression of the values of this world – sociability, inclusion and neighbourliness – his disdain for them is read as a rejection of these values.

Issues of public conduct also emerge in relation to Jane and Bingley's relationship, which is conducted in a public arena and subjected to the scrutiny of their family, friends and neighbours. Darcy's inability to discern sufficient emotion in Jane leads him to caution Bingley against pursuing a relationship with her. However, the open expression of emotion in this society is also critiqued with responses to Mrs Bennet's and Lydia's public performances. Elizabeth is frequently discomfited by the behaviour of her family in social settings. At the Netherfield ball in Chapter 18, the narrative notes that Elizabeth 'blushed and blushed again with shame and vexation' at her mother's loud criticisms of Darcy (p.97B; p.112R) and then is 'in agonies' at Mary's singing and desire for self-display (p.98B; p.112R).

An important aspect of the public self is *reputation*. An individual's reputation can be compromised not only by their own behaviour but by that of their family members. In Chapter 41, Elizabeth responds with anxiety when Mrs Forster invites Lydia to accompany her and the regiment to Brighton. Elizabeth's concerns are not only for Lydia herself but for the reflections the younger girl's behaviour casts on the rest of the family. Elizabeth's language in this chapter is marked by expectations of real danger: note her use of words such as 'evils', 'danger' and 'disgrace' (p.223B; pp.255–6R). Ultimately, the entire Lydia–Wickham affair demonstrates the precariousness of reputation in this world. In Chapter 46, she interprets Darcy's silence on the matter as proof of his disgust at her sister's behaviour. She feels so much shame that she does not blame him at all. In fact, it is only in this moment – when she feels that any chance of a relationship is utterly lost – that she realises 'she could have loved him' (p.264B; 304R).

DIFFERENT INTERPRETATIONS

Different interpretations arise from different responses to a text. Over time, a text will give rise to a wide range of responses from its readers, who may come from various social or cultural groups and live in very different places and historical periods. These responses can be published in newspapers, journals and books by critics and reviewers, or they can be expressed in discussions among readers in the media, classrooms, book groups and so on. While there is no single correct reading or interpretation of a text, it is important to understand that an interpretation is more than an 'opinion' – it is the justification of a point of view on the text. To present an interpretation of the text based on your point of view you must use a logical argument and support it with relevant evidence from the text.

Critical viewpoints

Austen's writing was popular with readers but did not receive much critical acclaim in her lifetime. The novels received mixed responses from critics and other writers in the 19th century. Whilst Sir Walter Scott praised Austen's presentation of the everyday realities of life, Charlotte Brontë found the works lifeless and lacking in real warmth and feeling (Morrison 2005, pp.51–2). A biographical study of Austen by her nephew in 1870 renewed interest in her work. This was demonstrated by the publication, in 1882, of the first collected edition of her novels. In the late 19th century, publishing houses also began to make cheaper single volumes of the novels available, thereby extending access to Austen's writing.

As Austen's works gained in popularity among general readers they also received increased scrutiny from academics and critics. These readers assessed the works in terms of their formal properties (including structure, narrative voice and the use of irony); their connection to their historical period; and their moral qualities. The late 20th century witnessed even greater interest in Austen's novels. From the 1970s onwards, *Pride and Prejudice* was read from a range of critical perspectives and points of focus, and analysed in terms of issues such as education, gender and sexuality, politics and religion. According to Robert Morrison, critical responses to the novel debated whether Austen 'capitulated to the power structures of patriarchy and aristocracy, or whether she defied these structures in favour of self-assertion, [middle-class] aspiration, and the dignity of women' (Morrison 2005, p.53).

The 20th century also saw the rise of 'Austeniana' – literary sequels and adaptations of her writings; theatre, film and television versions of the novels; and a growing heritage industry responding to the interest in Austen and her work. Her former home was established as an Austen museum, and a whole range of merchandise depicting Austen's image or quotes from her work continues to be produced. 'Austen obsession' has even become a subject of representation in itself. Texts such as Helen Fielding's Bridget Jones series and the telemovie *Lost in Austen* reflect and enhance this interest, particularly among younger women readers. Interestingly, *Pride and Prejudice* is the work most often identified in these examples. Thus the protagonist of *Lost in Austen* finds herself transported from the modern world into the Bennet household. And Bridget Jones' principal love interest is named Mark Darcy. Austen's Darcy and Fielding's Darcy were brought explicitly together in the public consciousness because the same actor (Colin Firth) was cast in both the BBC television series of *Pride and Prejudice* and the later film adaptations of the Bridget Jones books. *Pride and Prejudice* also repeatedly features in lists of favourite novels in many nations. In 2004 it was ranked number two in ABC television's 'My Favourite Book' survey.

It is interesting to consider the basis for this writer's continued popularity and the singular position of *Pride and Prejudice* among Austen's writings. Much of the novel's popularity is due, no doubt, to its status as the lightest and most obviously comic of Austen's works. We can also point to the 'fairytale romance' aspect of Elizabeth and Darcy's relationship and to the originality and charm of Elizabeth Bennet as a character. Austen herself remarked of the latter: 'I must confess that *I* think her as delightful a creature as ever appeared in print, and how I shall be able to tolerate those who do not like *her* at least, I do not know' (Tomalin 1997, p.221).

Film and television adaptations

Pride and Prejudice has been a popular text for adaptation. There have been over a dozen film and television adaptations of the novel as well as stage plays and musicals. When analysing adaptations of Austen's novels, we need to consider the influence of factors such as the demands of the medium and the need to attract viewers. A key aspect of *Pride and Prejudice* that is typically lost in translation to theatre and film is the narrator's ironic commentary on events. Directors and screenwriters must find other means for activating the ironic effect.

We also need to read film and television adaptations in terms of contemporary attitudes to Austen, as well as broader cultural preoccupations and prejudices. For example, the 1940 film version of *Pride and Prejudice*, starring Greer Garson and Laurence Olivier, was made at the outbreak of World War II. At a time when the contemporary world seemed frighteningly unstable, this film offered a romanticised vision of a gentler, more elegant world into which to escape. In order to achieve this vision, the film made some significant changes to the original plot. These included letting Lady Catherine give her blessing to Darcy's marriage before his proposal; and lessening Elizabeth's embarrassment towards her family, thereby removing the sense of her marriage as an escape from them. These changes allowed the film to present a reassuring portrait of family unity (Belton 2003, p.186).

Perhaps the best-known Austen adaptation is the 1995 BBC television version of *Pride and Prejudice*. It was phenomenally popular and provoked 'Darcymania' around the world, due at least partly to Colin Firth's smouldering performance. This version aimed to remain true to Austen's original whilst enhancing audience interest through the use of spectacular settings and scenery. It also laid particular emphasis on the romance between Elizabeth and Darcy. As Ellen Belton notes, this version closes with their 'long-awaited kiss', an ending that 'confirms the primacy of the romantic relationship' (Belton 2003, p.186).

The fluidity of Austen adaptations is demonstrated by Gurinder Chadha's 2004 film *Bride and Prejudice*. This film relocated the action of the novel to India and incorporated elements of Bollywood cinema traditions in its presentation. It brought new resonance to the original by adding anxiety about cultural difference to that of class difference: Lalita (Elizabeth) is Indian and 'Will' Darcy is American.

Two interpretations

Reading 1

Pride and Prejudice **supports women's use of marriage as a means of improving their social and financial status.**

This statement asks you to consider the novel's attitude to marriages based on economic or social considerations. A response to this statement requires an understanding of the nature of marriage in Austen's time. Why was there such an emphasis on marriage in a woman's life? How much control did a woman have in her choice of partner?

Several elements of *Pride and Prejudice* support this reading of the text. For example, Charlotte Lucas is obviously one of the more intelligent and level-headed characters in the novel, as demonstrated by her own dialogue and demeanour and by her status as Elizabeth's best friend. Her decision to marry the ridiculous Mr Collins is represented as a sensible choice for a woman in her situation. It allows her to finally leave the stifling environment of the parental home and establish her own household. Marrying a less-than-ideal partner offers her greater freedom than remaining dependent on her parents or, at some later point, her brothers.

The only person to significantly criticise Charlotte's choice is Elizabeth. Yet after spending time with the couple at Hunsford parsonage, she is forced to admit that her friend seems content. In any case, Elizabeth is perhaps not entirely qualified to make judgements about other people's marriages; her own decisions to reject Mr Collins and Darcy appear somewhat reckless considering her family's precarious financial position and her status as one of five dependent daughters.

The ending of *Pride and Prejudice* also supports the above reading. The text ultimately rewards Jane and Elizabeth, the two most attractive characters in the novel, with extremely advantageous marriages. By marrying Bingley and Darcy the oldest Bennet daughters are propelled towards the top of the social hierarchy and guaranteed futures of comfort and security. The novel's intense focus on Pemberley and its attractions, and the pleasure Elizabeth takes in the house and grounds, ensures the reader is fully aware of what the heroine gains through her marriage.

Reading 2

Pride and Prejudice **suggests the only happy marriages are those based on love and personal compatibility.**

This interpretation of the text considers the novel's representation of marriage, but also focuses more on issues of characterisation than of social context.

Several aspects of the novel support this reading. For example, we are constantly reminded of Mr Collins' unattractive qualities. At no point is the sense of Charlotte's incompatibility with her husband allowed to wane. Even though she seems satisfied with her life at Hunsford, there is certainly no indication that hers and Mr Collins' is a 'happy' marriage.

The novel can be read as delighting in Elizabeth's spirit when she rejects Mr Collins and Darcy, rather than critiquing her recklessness. In these terms her actions can be interpreted to suggest self-determination is more valuable to a woman than a comfortable but loveless union.

Several of the marriages in *Pride and Prejudice* are shown to be based on factors other than love and personal compatibility. The most striking example is the marriage of Mr and Mrs Bennet, of which the novel performs an extended critique. This couple's inability to communicate or even demonstrate sensitivity towards one another is clearly shown. The unfortunate union has stunted the personal development of both Mr and Mrs Bennet, and it also has broader ramifications. Lydia's actions can be read as a response to the model of marriage with which she has been presented. There is even the suggestion that the Bennet marriage resulted from the same kind of unchecked sexual desire that prompted Lydia and Wickham to run away together. The fortunes of the latter couple show the novel critiquing unions based on sexual attraction rather than love and compatibility. In Chapter 61 we are informed that Lydia and Wickham are subjected to a restless, unsettled existence and soon grow apart. In comparison, Jane and Elizabeth are fulfilled by their respective marriages.

QUESTIONS & ANSWERS

This section focuses on your own analytical writing on the text, and gives you strategies for producing high-quality responses in your coursework and exam essays.

Essay topics

1 How do the five Bennet sisters reflect the different values and attitudes of women at this time?

2 'Despite their apparent differences, there are significant similarities between Elizabeth and both her mother and youngest sister.' Discuss.

3 'Elizabeth Bennet considers herself a better judge of character than she actually is.' Discuss.

4 Elizabeth observes to Darcy, "your defect is a propensity to hate every body" and Darcy replies, "And yours ... is to wilfully misunderstand them". Do you agree with Elizabeth's and Darcy's assessments of each other?

5 Darcy says to Elizabeth, "We neither of us perform to strangers". Do you agree with Darcy?

6 'Elizabeth's responses to Pemberley reflect her changing attitude to Darcy himself.' Discuss.

7 'Pride and Prejudice supports women's use of marriage as a means of improving their social and financial status.' Do you agree?

8 'Pride and Prejudice shows that class is not an accurate indicator of character.' Discuss.

9 'Austen uses comedy to mock some characters, but to show sympathy and affection for others.'

10 How does comedy influence your response to characters in Pride and Prejudice?

11 Discuss the importance of letters in the narrative. How do they enhance our understanding of character and/or move the narrative forward?

Vocabulary for writing on *Pride and Prejudice*

Realist novel: this type of novel reflects the real world of the author. It presents recognisable characters and true-to-life situations.

Omniscient narrator: a narrative voice that comments on the action and has complete knowledge of all the characters' thoughts and feelings.

Free indirect discourse: a style in which the narrative voice seems to reflect the thoughts and feelings of a particular character. For example, when Elizabeth tells Darcy of Lydia's departure with Wickham, the narrative expresses her interpretation of his reaction to the news: 'Her power was sinking; every thing must sink under such a proof of family weakness, such an assurance of the deepest disgrace' (p.264B; p.304R).

Satire: the use of comic techniques to ridicule folly, vice or pretension. By comically exaggerating Mr Collins' obsequiousness and Lady Catherine's arrogance, *Pride and Prejudice* satirises these characters' attitudes to class.

Irony: the use of language to suggest an implied meaning directly opposite to the surface meaning.

Foreshadowing: the use of hints and clues to the reader to suggest future developments. For example, in Chapter 32 Darcy tests Elizabeth's views on whether a married woman need live close to her family. The reason for his questioning will become clear following his proposal to her in Chapter 34.

Analysing a sample topic

'Despite their apparent differences, there are significant similarities between Elizabeth Bennet and both her mother and youngest sister.' Discuss.

This question asks you to closely consider the attitudes, values and behaviours of three characters in the novel: Elizabeth Bennet, Mrs Bennet and Lydia Bennet. It asks you to examine the traits and behaviours Elizabeth shares with her mother and sister and to assess the significance of these in understanding her attitudes and actions. The essay question expects you to consider both similarities *and* differences.

You need to formulate a main contention, or a central response to the topic. For this question, you might decide to agree that Elizabeth actually has many things in common with Mrs Bennet and Lydia. Your main contention could be: 'Elizabeth shares a number of important traits with her mother and youngest sister, and these qualities govern many of her actions'. A more complex main contention is given in the final sentence of the following sample introduction.

Sample introduction

> *Pride and Prejudice* celebrates Elizabeth Bennet's independent outlook and unconventional spirit. At first glance she seems to have little in common with the other members of her family, and it makes sense that she ultimately leaves Longbourn for the very different world of Pemberley. However, upon closer examination it becomes apparent that Elizabeth shares a number of traits and attitudes with Mrs Bennet and Lydia, and her awareness of these similarities produces in her significant levels of discomfort and anxiety.

Paragraph outline

Paragraph 1: The first paragraph should outline the apparent differences between Elizabeth and Mrs Bennet/Lydia.

* Elizabeth seems to exhibit more common sense than either Mrs Bennet or Lydia.
* Elizabeth appears to be a better judge of character.
* Elizabeth exhibits greater self-control and propriety in public.

The next three paragraphs should identify and analyse aspects of Elizabeth's character that complicate the above observations.

Paragraphs 2 and 3: Discuss character traits Elizabeth shares with Mrs Bennet/Lydia. Aspects of the text that could be drawn on include the following.

* Elizabeth shares her mother and sister's enthusiasm, and delight in fun and laughter. There are repeated references to Lydia's laughter and Elizabeth herself admits: 'I dearly love a laugh' (p.56B; p.62R).
* There are repeated references to Mrs Bennet's and Lydia's talkative natures and the novel includes passages of their long, rambling conversations (see, for example, page 213). On her visit to Jane and Elizabeth at Netherfield Park, Mrs Bennet suggests Elizabeth shares this tendency: 'Lizzy … remember where you are, and do not run on in the wild manner that you are suffered to do at home' (p.42B; pp.46–7R).

* Unlike Mr Bennet, who retreats to his library, and the more home-loving Jane and Mary, these three characters are outward-focused and interested in new experiences. Elizabeth travels to Hunsford and Pemberley, whilst Lydia journeys to Brighton and Mrs Bennet expresses a desire that she could go also (p.221B; p.253R).

* Elizabeth realises she, like her mother and sister, is capable of improper behaviour in public. In Chapter 36 she regrets encouraging Wickham's confidences about Darcy and recognises she has indulged in the kind of impropriety she had herself criticised in Lydia.

Paragraph 4: Identify attitudes to others shared by Elizabeth and Mrs Bennet/Lydia.

* All three characters are sociable and enjoy other people's company. Lydia's ecstatic responses to social invitations are not unlike Elizabeth's excited reaction to the proposed holiday with Mr and Mrs Gardiner.

* Elizabeth and Mrs Bennet reject class distinctions. Elizabeth is not intimidated by Lady Catherine and stands up to her. Mrs Bennet dislikes Darcy and is openly rude to him despite his wealth and status.

* All three characters are easily influenced by first impressions. They are all attracted to, and ultimately deceived by, Wickham's apparent charms.

Sample conclusion

A close reading of *Pride and Prejudice* exposes the traits and attitudes Elizabeth shares with her mother and youngest sister. Like Mrs Bennet and Lydia, Elizabeth possesses the desire for laughter, new friends and new experiences. These yearnings at times lead all three characters to make rash judgements and Elizabeth learns that she is not exempt from some of her family's faults and failings. She expresses more discomfort in relation to her mother and sister than to any other characters in the novel. This discomfort stems in part from her awareness of the characteristics she shares with them. Much of Elizabeth's delight in retreating to Pemberley arises from the distance it will place between her and her family, thus minimising the reminders they offer her of certain aspects of her own character.

An alternative argument

The above analysis assumes an agreement with the proposition. It is also possible to argue that Elizabeth is in fact very different from Mrs Bennet and Lydia, or that the characteristics she shares with her mother and sister are not particularly significant. In order to develop a main contention which argues *against* the essay topic, you might examine points including the following:

* Elizabeth's sensitivity and intelligence, which distance her from Mrs Bennet and Lydia

* Elizabeth's similarities with Mr Bennet and Jane – you might argue that her humour has more in common with that of her father than her mother or sister, and that her behaviour in public is closer to Jane's than Lydia's

* Elizabeth's ability to reassess her initial impressions, which gives her a different outlook on the world from her mother or sister.

SAMPLE ANSWER

'Elizabeth's responses to Pemberley reflect her changing attitude to Darcy himself.' Discuss.

In *Pride and Prejudice*, Elizabeth's visit to Pemberley with the Gardiners in Volume Three is presented as a key event in the development of her relationship with Darcy. In the novel, Pemberley stands in for Darcy himself; all of its features are a reflection of his values and attitudes. Before his sudden appearance in person, Elizabeth is able to assess the estate and the judgements of its housekeeper. She is surprised and delighted at the style of the house and its grounds, and impressed by Mrs Reynolds' assessments of Darcy as employer, estate owner and brother to Georgiana. Her experience of Pemberley allows Elizabeth to be intimate with Darcy even whilst he is absent, and encourages her to reconsider her understanding of his character.

The visit to Pemberley follows Darcy's first proposal of marriage, which Elizabeth wholeheartedly rejects. Her rejection is motivated by his arrogant assessment of their differing class positions, and by her understanding of his interference in Jane and Bingley's relationship and in Wickham's career prospects. However, Darcy's letter responding to her charges prompts Elizabeth to doubt some of her previous impressions, particularly those concerning Wickham. Whilst the letter opens Elizabeth's mind to an alternative appreciation of events, it is the visit to Pemberley that causes her to significantly reassess her first impressions of Darcy's character.

At the close of Volume Two, Elizabeth expresses curiosity about Pemberley. Her excitement at this visit is indicated by the opening paragraph of Volume Three, which notes that 'her spirits were in a high flutter' as they approached the estate. She only agrees to go, however, upon being assured that Darcy himself will not be present. Elizabeth presumes therefore that the visit will enable her to indulge her curiosity about Darcy's world without having to engage with the man himself. In fact, she will be surprised by his sudden appearance, but this only happens towards the end of the visit and once she has had her views of his character challenged by her experience of the estate.

One of the first things Elizabeth notes about Pemberley is its simple, understated elegance. The grounds lack artificiality and the banks of the stream are 'neither formal, nor falsely adorned'. Elizabeth was unimpressed by the opulent, ostentatious grandeur of Lady Catherine's estate, Rosings Park, but she immediately responds to the natural beauty of Pemberley. Furthermore, she connects her admiration for the estate with a possible relationship with its owner: 'at that moment she felt that to be mistress of Pemberley might be something'. Through this visit she learns that her tastes are in accord with those of Darcy.

As she is struck by the grounds, Elizabeth is also pleasantly surprised by Mrs Reynolds, the housekeeper of Pemberley: a woman 'much less fine, and more civil, than she had any notion of finding her'. The furnishings of the house are also less 'uselessly fine' and more elegant than those of Rosings Park. By this point it has become apparent to Elizabeth that Darcy holds a very different attitude to wealth and its expression than his aunt does, and it is an attitude of which Elizabeth herself approves.

Mrs Reynolds conducts the party around the house and volunteers information about Darcy's attentiveness to his sister, generosity to the poor, and kindness to his tenants and employees. Elizabeth is particularly impressed by the housekeeper's comments regarding her master's temper. Mrs Reynolds notes she has 'never had a cross word from him' in her life: praise that Elizabeth acknowledges is 'most opposite to her ideas'. By the time she comes face to face with a portrait of Darcy at the end of the tour, Elizabeth feels 'a more gentle sensation towards the original' than she has at any previous point in their acquaintance. Later in the novel, when her engagement has been confirmed, Elizabeth tells Jane that she believes her love for Darcy must date from 'first seeing his beautiful grounds at Pemberley'. She means this as a joke, playing on the notion that she is primarily attracted to his wealth and status, but there seems a deeper truth in her jest.

It is Darcy's letter, responding to Elizabeth's claims justifying her refusal of his marriage proposal, that challenges her initial assumptions about his attitudes and actions. Yet it is her experience of Pemberley that significantly furthers her reassessment of his character. Her delight in the unaffected beauty of the house and grounds suggests their shared taste, whilst the testimony of Mrs Reynolds contradicts Elizabeth's earlier understanding of Darcy's personal qualities. The experience of Pemberley prepares Elizabeth for the changes she discerns in Darcy when he suddenly appears in person; this encourages her to negotiate a new mode of relating to him, and eventually contributes to her decision to marry him.

REFERENCES & READING

Text

Austen, Jane 2003, *Pride and Prejudice*, Penguin Classics, London. (B)
——2006, *Pride and Prejudice*, Penguin, London. (R)

Films

Pride and Prejudice 1940, dir. Robert Z. Leonard, MGM. Starring Greer Garson and Laurence Olivier.
Pride and Prejudice 1995, dir. Simon Langton, BBC. Starring Jennifer Ehle and Colin Firth.
Bride and Prejudice 2004, dir. Gurinder Chadha, Miramax Films. Starring Aishwarya Rai and Martin Henderson.

Websites

The Jane Austen Society of Australia, www.jasa.net.au
The Jane Austen Society of North America, www.jasna.org
The Republic of Pemberley, www.pemberley.com

Other references

Belton, Ellen 2003, 'Reimagining Jane Austen: The 1940 and 1995 Film Versions of *Pride and Prejudice*', in Gina Macdonald and Andrew Macdonald (eds), *Jane Austen on Screen*, Cambridge University Press, Cambridge, pp.175–96.

Irvine, Robert P. 2005, *Jane Austen*, Routledge, London.

Kelly, Gary 1989, *English Fiction of the Romantic Period, 1789–1830*, Longman, London.

McMaster, Juliet 1997, 'Class', in Edward Copeland and Juliet McMaster, eds, *The Cambridge Companion to Jane Austen*, Cambridge University Press, Cambridge, pp.115–30.

Morrison, Robert 2005, *Jane Austen's Pride and Prejudice: A Sourcebook*, Routledge, London.

Olsen, Kristin 2005, *All Things Austen: An Encyclopedia of Austen's World, Volume 2, M–Z*, Greenwood Press, Connecticut.

Sutherland, John and LeFaye, Deirdre 2005, *So You Think You Know Jane Austen?*, Oxford University Press, Oxford.

Tanner, Tony 1986, *Jane Austen*, Macmillan, Houndmills, Basingstoke.

Tomalin, Claire 1997, *Jane Austen: A Life*, Viking, London.

notes

CPSIA information can be obtained at www.ICGtesting.com
Printed in the USA
LVOW071437231212

312975LV00001B/130/P

9 781921 411410

[5]